# ART
# TREASURES
## OF THE
# VATICAN

*Bergomi, 30 Julii 1950*

Perlibenter licentiam facimus ut hoc opus edatur quod « Institutum Italicum Artis Graphicæ », vertente Anno Sancto, egregie imprimendum curavit, ad illustrandum quam sedule Apostolica Sedes, in Dei gloriam, semper bonas artes foverit.

† A. BERNAREGGI
*Episcopus*

# BARTOLOMEO NOGARA

DIRECTOR GENERAL OF THE PONTIFICAL MONUMENTS, MUSEUMS AND GALLERIES

# ART
# TREASURES
## OF THE
# VATICAN

TUDOR PUBLISHING COMPANY - NEW YORK

ISTITUTO ITALIANO D'ARTI GRAFICHE - BERGAMO (ITALY)

# SUMMARY

# SUMARIO

# SOMMAIRE

# SOMMARIO

# INTRODUCTION

*The name Vatican is familiar today to every person of culture all over the world, and yet in ancient times it merely signified a small hill between Mt. Marius and the Janiculum, with an adjoining plain along the right bank of the Tiber where various Roman families had their tombs. It is true that a circus was erected there by the two Emperors, Caligula (37-41 A. D.) and Nero (54-68). But only a few specialists of ancient topography would now remember its name if the persecution of the early Christians which took place there had not included among its victims the first Vicar of Christ, the Apostle Peter; and if among the tombs which lie along the Via Cornelia there had not been his Sepulcher. This Sepulcher was made up of two rooms, one above the other: the lower one destined for the crypt itself, the top one as a place where the faithful could meet, even though only in private, to honor the memory of their leader and his immediate successors. With the victory of Constantine over Maxentius (312) and the proclamation of the freedom of the Church at Milan (313), the situation changed. It was then that the great Basilicas were built, and first among them the Lateran, as the Cathedral of Rome, and the Vatican, as the Cathedral of all Christianity. The Vatican, which housed the remains of the First Apostle, had a certain character of priority which assured it a preference in the worship and veneration of the whole Christian world. Alongside the Basilica arose the homes of the ecclesiastics who officiated there; later, those of the Popes who went there on great solemn occasions until, during the fifteenth century, they moved in permanently. The Christian Emperors, and above all Constantine the Great, did everything possible to enrich with gold, silver and precious ornaments the tomb of the First Apostle and his Basilica. The power and prestige thus acquired by the Vatican enabled it to withstand two centuries of invasions by plundering barbarians, and in the end to disarm and convert them, not by force, but by the sole power of its doctrine and charity. This wise work of the Popes, of whom Gregory the Great (590-604) was the most brilliant example, carried out during the darkest centuries of the Middle Ages, made of the Vatican a great artistic center which is unique in the world.*

# INTRODUCCIÓN

*No hay persona de alguna cultura que nunca haya oido hablar del Vaticano. En la edad clásica este nombre indicaba una modesta colina entre Monte Mario y el Janículo, con una zona casi llana a la derecha del Tíber, atravesada por la Via Cornelia, que muchas familias romanas habían escojido para sus tumbas.*

*Dos Emperadores, Calígula (37-41 d. de J. C.) y Nerón (54-68) habían edificado aqui un circo, pero no más que unos pocos estudiosos de topografía antigua recordarían hoy su nombre si en este sitio, entre las primeras víctimas de las persecuciones contra los Cristianos, no hubiera sido el primer Vicario de Jesucristo, el Apóstol Pedro, y si entre las tumbas que flanqueaban la Via Cornelia, no hubiera tenido él su sepulcro. Estaba compuesta la tumba de S. Pedro de dos cuartos, uno encima del otro; lo de abajo estaba destinado al sepulcro, y lo de arriba a la reunión de los fieles, que podían congregarse, aún en forma privada, para venerar la memoria de su Jefe y de Sus inmediatos sucesores. Pero esta situación acabó con la victoria de Constantino sobre Majencio al Puente Milvio (312) y con la proclamación de la libertad de la Iglesia (edicto de Milán, en 313). En este período edificáronse las grandes Basílicas, como la de San Juán de Letrán y la del Vaticano; la primera es la catedral de Roma, mientras que la segunda es la catedral de toda la cristiandad; y esta, que guardaba a los despojos del primer Vicario de Jesucristo, tuvo un carácter de prioridad que le aseguró la preferencia en la veneración y en el culto de todo el mundo cristiano. Al lado de la Basílica fueron edificadas las moradas de los eclesiásticos que la custodiaban, luego las de los Pontífices que la visitaban en ocasión de las grandes solemnidades y que acabaron por establecer allí definitivamente su residencia en el siglo XV. Los emperadores cristianos, empezando con Constantino Iº, compitieron en enriquecer con oro, plata y arreos preciosos la tumba del Príncipe de los Apóstoles y su Basílica; y aún por dos siglos los invasores barbáricos tratasen de arrancar de su frente la guirnalda gloriosa con que las había ceñidas la piedad de los fieles, el Vaticano, no más con la fuerza, sino con el poder pacífico de la doctrina y de la caridad, consiguió desarmarlos y convertirlos. Esta fué la obra prudente del Papado en los siglos más obscuros de la Edad Media, de que Gregorio Iº Magno (590-604) dió el ejemplo más luminoso, y que hizo del Vaticano un centro artístico y monumental único en el mundo.*

# INTRODUCTION

Il n'est personne doué d'un minimum d'instruction à qui le nom du Vatican soit étranger. Aux âges classiques, il désignait une modeste colline entre le Mont Marius et le Janicule, avec une zone basse et plate sur la rive droite du Tibre, à travers laquelle courait la Voie Cornélienne, et que maintes familles romaines avaient choisie pour leurs tombeaux. Deux empereurs, Caligula (37-41 après J. C.) et Néron (45-68), y avaient bâti un cirque ; mais seuls quelques savants férus de topographie ancienne se rappelleraient aujourd'hui ce nom, s'il ne s'était trouvé en ces lieux, parmi les victimes de la première persécution contre le chrétiens, le Vicaire du Christ, l'Apôtre Pierre, et s'il n'avait eu, parmi les tombeaux qui bordaient la Voie Cornélienne, sa sépulture. Elle se composait de deux chambres l'une au-dessus de l'autre, celle du bas destinée au sépulcre proprement dit, celle du haut à la réunion des fidèles, qui pouvaient se rassembler, mais en privé seulement, pour vénérer la mémoire de leur chef et de ses successeurs immédiats. Mais cet était de choses prit fin avec la victoire de Constantin sur Maxime au Pont Milvius (312), et la proclamation de la liberté de l'Eglise à Milan (313). C'est alors que surgirent les grandes Basiliques, et d'abord celles du Latran et du Vatican. Deux basiliques primatiales : comme cathédrale de Rome la première ; de toute la chrétienté, la seconde. Et celle-ci, parce quelle conservait la dépouille du premier Vicaire du Christ, eut un caractère de priorité qui lui assura la préférence dans le culte et la vénération de tout le monde chrétien. Auprès de la Basilique s'élevèrent les habitations des ecclésiastiques desservants, puis celles des Pontifes qui s'y rendaient à l'occasion des grandes solennités, jusqu'au XVe siècle où ils s'y établirent à demeure. Les empereurs chrétiens, et, le premier de tous, Constantin le Grand, avaient rivalisé entre eux pour enrichir d'or, d'argent et d'ornements précieux le tombeau du Prince des Apôtres et sa basilique, et bien que durant deux siècles les Barbares envahisseurs eussent essayé de leur arracher du front la glorieuse couronne dont les avait ceints la piété des fidèles, toujours le Vatican était parvenu à les désarmer et à les convertir non par la force, mais par la vertu pacifique de la doctrine et de la charité.

Au cours des siècles les plus sombres du Moyen âge telle fut la tâche du Pontificat dont Grégoire le Grand (590-604) a donné le plus éclatant exemple, et qui a fait du Vatican un centre artistique et monumental unique au monde.

# INTRODUZIONE

Non c'è persona di qualche cultura a cui giunga nuovo il nome del Vaticano. Esso indicava nell'età classica una modesta collina tra Monte Mario e il Gianicolo, con una zona pianeggiante sulla destra del Tevere, attraversata dalla Via Cornelia e che parecchie famiglie romane avevano scelto per le loro tombe.

Due imperatori, Caligola (37-41 dopo C.) e Nerone (54-68) vi avevano eretto un circo; ma soltanto pochi studiosi di topografia antica ne ricorderebbero ora il nome, se in questa località, tra le vittime della prima persecuzione contro i Cristiani, non vi fosse stato il primo Vicario di Cristo, l'Apostolo Pietro, e se tra le tombe, che fiancheggiavano la Via Cornelia, egli non avesse avuto la sua sepoltura. Essa si componeva di due camere, l'una sopra l'altra: l'inferiore destinata al sepolcro vero e proprio, la superiore alla riunione dei fedeli, i quali potevano adunarsi, benchè solo in forma privata, per venerare la memoria del loro capo e dei suoi immediati successori. Ma questo stato di cose cessò con la vittoria di Costantino su Massenzio a Ponte Milvio (312) e con la proclamazione della libertà della Chiesa a Milano (313). Allora sorsero le grandi basiliche, e prime tra esse quelle del Laterano e del Vaticano; due basiliche di primato, come cattedrale di Roma, la prima, come cattedrale, la seconda, di tutta la cristianità; e questa, che conservava le spoglie del primo Vicario di Cristo, ebbe un carattere di priorità, che le assicurò la preferenza nella venerazione e nel culto di tutto il mondo cristiano. Accanto alla Basilica sorsero le abitazioni degli ecclesiastici che la custodivano, poi quelle dei Pontefici che vi si recavano in occasione delle grandi solennità, fino a che nel secolo XV essi vi trasferirono stabilmente la loro dimora. Gl'imperatori cristiani, e, primo fra tutti, Costantino Magno, avevano gareggiato fra loro nell'arricchire d'oro, d'argento e di arredi preziosi la tomba del Principe degli Apostoli e la sua basilica, e sebbene per due secoli i barbari invasori avessero tentato strappar loro dalla fronte il serto glorioso di cui le aveva recinte la pietà dei fedeli, il Vaticano, non più con la forza, ma col potere pacifico della dottrina e della carità, era riuscito a disarmarli e a convertirli. Questa era stata l'opera sapiente del Pontificato nei secoli più oscuri del Medio Evo, di cui Gregorio Magno (590-604) diede il più luminoso esempio, e che ha fatto del Vaticano un centro artistico e monumentale unico al mondo.

12

Aerial View of Vatican City.   The Basilica, extending from East to West, with the two lateral porticoes of Constantine on the right and of Charlemagne on the left and with the elliptical colonnades, forms the central nucleus; toward the North are the Palaces, which consist of various buildings located principally around the courts of San Damaso, Belvedere and Pigna.

La Ciudad del Vaticano vista del avión: la Basílica está dispuesta de este a oeste, con el pórtico lateral de Constantino a la derecha y el pórtico lateral de Carlomagno a la izquierda y la columnata elíptica. La Basílica constituye el núcleo central del conjunto. Al norte están los Palacios divididos en distintos edificios, que se desarrollan especialmente alrededor del patio de San Damaso y a los patios de Belvedere y de la Piña.

Vue aérienne de la Cité du  Vatican. La Basilique orientée d'E en O, avec les deux porches latéraux de Constantin à droite et de Carlemagne à  gauche et avec la colonnade elliptique, forme le noyau central: vers le nord il y a les palais subdivisés en plusieurs bâtiments, qui se développent principalement autour de la cour de S. Damase et des bâtiments du Belvédère et de la « Pigna ».

Veduta aerea della Città del Vaticano. La Basilica orientata da E. ad O., con i due portici laterali di Costantino a destra e di Carlo Magno a sinistra e con il colonnato ellittico forma il nucleo centrale: verso N. sono i palazzi suddivisi in diversi fabbricati, che si sviluppano principalmente intorno al cortile di S. Damaso ed a quelli del Belvedere e della Pigna.

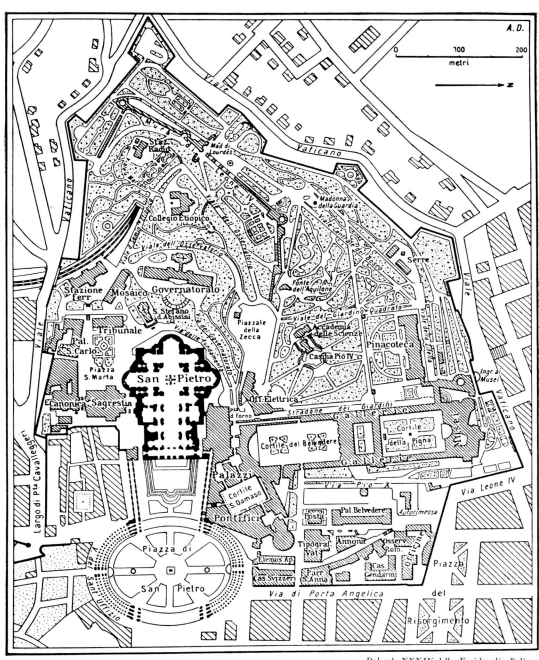

Plan of Vatican City - Plantilla de la Ciudad del Vaticano
Plan de la Cité du Vatican - Pianta della Città del Vaticano

THE BASILICA

LA BASÍLICA

LA BASILIQUE

LA BASILICA

As we said in the beginning, only the Vatican Basilica survived the immense confusion which accompanied the fall of the Roman Empire, when so many treasures of ancient civilization were dispersed or destroyed. By restoring rapidly the losses endured, it became a new center of attraction for all peoples. Not many years had passed since the invasions of the Goths, led by Alaric (410), and of the Vandals, led by Genseric (455), when other barbarians came from the North through the old consular roads. But these were not carrying arms or shouting battle cries, and were not contemplating massacre, fire and ruin; these were holding the Cross on high and singing sacred hymns. They were coming to kneel at the foot of an altar, before an old priest, seeking his benediction: they had stripped themselves of their riches in order to lay them on the tomb of the First Apostle. Thus it was that new groups of Angles, Franks, Saxons and Friesians, heirs of the ancient invaders, returned to Rome as to the honored mother of the nations. Then the temple of the Vatican had nothing more to envy the Capitol, extolled by Horace at the time of its glory, when it was resplendent with conquered arms and with gold brought from distant provinces. From Rome, sent by Gregory the Great, large numbers of monks set out for Germany, led by St. Boniface; others, led by St. Augustine, set out for England. These monks, in order to compensate for the losses suffered through the menacing advance of Islam, were to acquire for the Church new throngs of faithful followers and would entrust them with the preservation in manuscripts of the best that ancient civilization had left as a heritage. Two centuries later, in St. Peter's Basilica, on Christmas night of the year 800, Charles, King of the Franks, was to be crowned Emperor amid the acclamations of the people to « Charles, the most pious, crowned by God, great and peaceful Emperor ». Rome, as the home of the Vatican, was becoming the seat of a new universal domination, that of the Holy Roman Empire.

17

The benefits of this great event, while extended gradually to the whole Christian world, were felt, as was natural, especially in Rome and in the Vatican, where the warlike power of the Caesars was replaced by the peaceful power of the Popes: their temporal rule, which lasted but a few centuries, was only a pale reflection of their increasing authority and prestige. This movement became also a powerful appeal for uniting the nations in peace, under the sponsorship of the two great powers of society, the Church and the State. It is true that this ideal was never fully attained; still, despite countless problems and difficulties, it yielded incalculable benefits. For the first time it was understood that the Christian nations, although divided by race, language and traditions, were called upon to form a single family and to collaborate for the common interests of civilization. Moreover, it was possible, with the passage of time, to resolve the quarrel of the « Investitures », to launch the Crusades which reopened the East to the West, and to foster the legal, philosophical, theological and literary movement, out of which came the *Decretum* of Graziano, the *Summa Theologica* of St. Thomas, the Comedy of Dante, as well as the renaissance of arts and sciences on which modern civilization is nourished.

It is easy, therefore, to explain how and why everyone turned to the Vatican, the Basilica and the Holy See: the admirers of the classic world, the worshipers of old Christian memories, the pilgrims, the artists and the scholars; and with them came most precious gifts, destined to enrich the monuments and to bear testimony to the veneration and affection of all believers. To this movement, continuing through the centuries up to the present time, both the Basilica and the Vatican Palace owe the origin of their art treasures which are famed the world over. The Basilica, begun by Constantine in 324 and completed in 349, was to attract the best that the arts could offer in the glorious sunset of the Roman Empire. Historians of that time and the *Liber Pontificalis* give marvellous accounts of the treasures, but very little of the ancient riches of the Constantine period or of succeeding centuries was saved from destruction and theft. Among the treasures which do remain we may cite the following: a silver-gilt cross, studded with precious stones, gift of Justin II, Emperor of Constantinople, and his wife Sophia (570), which contains a piece of the True Cross; the so-called « dalmatica » of Charlemagne, a byzantine work of art of the fourteenth century, imported from Constantinople after its destruction (1453); an ancient statue of a philosopher, converted into one of St. Peter, which used to be in the Atrium and is now preserved in the Grottoes; the other statue in bronze, venerated in the Basilica; the mosaics of the Chapel of John VII (705-707); the tomb of Otto III (983) and that of Boniface VIII (1294-1305) which is attributed to Arnolfo di Cambio; the Giotto polyptych of Cardinal Stefaneschi (about 1300), made for the Papal Altar and now in the Vatican Pinacoteca. The original structure of the Basilica had always remained standing, but its condition had been rendered so dangerous by earthquakes, human neglect and, most of all, the ravages of time, that in the middle of the fifteenth century Pope Nicholas V (1447-1455) decided to reconstruct it. His death, however, interrupted the work when it was hardly begun, and fifty idle years passed before Julius II (1503-1513), taking up the idea again, entrusted its execution to Bramante. In 1506 the first stone was laid, but once again the death of the Pope (1513) and of the architect (1514) slowed up the work. Determined to delay no longer, Paul III had recourse to Michelangelo (1546), leaving him perfectly free to enlarge or transform the whole according to his own judgment. Michelangelo, despite his seventy-two years, accepted the commission and nobly refused any recompense. He went back to Bramante's design of a temple in the shape of a Greek cross, but instead of the Pantheon dome conceived by Bramante he designed another one, slightly narrower but of much greater height, inspired by Brunelleschi's dome at Florence. In order that his successors might have a sure guide in the continuation of the work he had a wooden model made under his own direction, which is still being preserved as a very interesting and precious object. Michelangelo died in 1564, before the work was finished; but Domenico Fontana and Giacomo Della Porta, with some slight modifications, brought the dome to completion (1590). Thus, to the seven hills of Rome a new one, greater and more majestic, was added: a symbol of unity, peace and hope, to which would turn all the pilgrims of the arts and of the faith.

A structure such as Michelangelo had planned would have been artistically the most perfect; but the necessity of enlarging the capacity of the temple could only be met by extending the building in the front, thus giving it the shape of a Latin cross. This addition, the portico and the façade were finished by the architect Maderno in 1614. Lorenzo Bernini, during the years 1656-1666, crowned the colossal work with the lateral wings of the portico and the colonnades around the square. The great equestrian statues of Constantine and Charlemagne at the ends of the lateral wings, where they reach the portico, were the guardian sentinels; and the hundred and forty statues of Martyrs and Confessors of the Faith, standing on top of the wings and the colonnades, were the chorus, singing perennially the hymns of glory to the Prince of the Apostles. Thus came to its final form an architectural monument which is unique in the world (see page 33).

On first entering the Basilica we are so struck by its grandiose proportions, that we cannot grasp at once the richness and infinite variety of the details (page 38).

We will mention here only the principal ones. Directly under Michelangelo's dome and beneath Bernini's Canopy (Baldacchino), inaugurated by Urban VIII in 1633, stands the Papal Altar (pages 35, 36, 40); beyond it, the Altar of the Cathedra Petri, also the work of Bernini (1658-1666), which with the Chair itself, the colossal figures of the doctors of the Church supporting it, the mystic dove of the window panes and the little angels who surround it, is in perfect harmony with the whole architectural structure (pages 41-43).

After these Altars, which are the chief centers of the Basilica, two others deserve consideration: the Altar of the Pietà, so named for the marble group in which Michelangelo (1498) transfused the intensity of his faith in the mystery of the Redemption (pages 44-46), and the Altar of the Blessed Sacrament, with its bronze-gilt tabernacle, a work of Bernini (1674-1675) which seems clearly inspired by Bramante's little temple on the Janiculum. Besides the Altars, we must mention some of the monuments and sepulchers which are among the finest works of sculpture of recent centuries, from the Renaissance to the present day: the monuments of Paul III by Guglielmo Della Porta (pages 47, 48), of Urban VIII by Bernini (page 49), of Clement XIII and of Pius VI by Canova. A second monument of Pius VI, at the head of the Sacristy staircase, a work in the baroque style but very effective, was modelled by Gaspare Sibilia and executed by Agostino Penna toward the end of the eighteenth century (page 51). Necessary complements to the Basilica are the Treasure, annexed to the Sacristy, and the Grottoes, a name for the subterranean part of the Constantine Basilica, where the relics of the Prince of the Apostles are preserved. In the Treasure we may admire the cross of the Emperor Justin and the « dalmatica » of Charlemagne, already mentioned above, and many fine examples of the minor arts, in gold and other materials, from the Middle Ages up to our days. In the Grottoes, besides the statue of St. Peter, the mosaics and the tombs of Otto and Boniface VIII, of which we have already spoken, we may admire the sepulcher of Sixtus IV (1471-1484) by Pollaiolo, considered the most perfect bronze work of the Italian Renaissance; and also the bas-reliefs and sculptures by Mino da Fiesole and Giovanni Dalmata, which formed the principal part of the tomb of Paul II (1464-1471) before it was dismantled at the time the old basilica was demolished.

Como ya dijemos arriba, en la desmedida perturbación que accompañó a la caída del Imperio Romano, cuando los tesoros acumulados por la civilización clásica fueron en su mayoría dispersos o aniquilados, tán solo la Basílica Vaticana sobrevivió, remediando rapidamente a sus pérdidas, y volviéndose un nuevo centro de atracción para todos los pueblos. Ya no habían pasado muchos años desde las incursiones de los Godos capitaneados por Alarico (410) y de los Vándalos guiados por Genserico (455), cuando más columnas de bárbaros se vieron llegar desde el Norte, recorriendo a las antiguas carreteras consulares; pero estos no llevaban armas, no cantaban cantos de guerra, no proyectaban matanzas, incendios y ruinas; levantaban altas las cruces y cantaban salmodias religiosas; venían ellos para arrodillarse a los piés de un altar, delante de un viejo sacerdote a quién ian pedir su bendición; habíanse despojado de sus riquezas para depornelas sobre la tumba del Príncipe del los Apóstoles. Volvieron así a Roma, como a la madre venerada de los pueblos, nuevas turbas de Anglios, de Francos, de Sajones, de Frisones, los herederos de los antiguos invasores; y el Vaticano nada más tuvo que envidiar al Capitolio que cantó Horacio, soberbio de armas conquistadas, fúlgido de mármoles y oros aunados en provincias lejanas. Y desde Roma, enviadas por Gregorio Magno, partiron legiones de monjes, guiados por San Bonifacio para Alemania y por San Augustín para Inglaterra, quienes, para compensar a las pérdidas sufridas por obra de la Media Luna, que se adelantaba ameazadora, adquirirán aquí a la Iglesia nuevas muchedumbres de fieles, a quienes confiarán para custodiar en los códigos la herencia más electa de la civilización clásica. Dos siglos más tarde, en la Basílica Vaticana, la noche de Navidad del año 800, Carlos, el Rey de los Francos, será coronado Emperador entre las aclamaciones del pueblo « a Carlos piísimo augusto, coronado por Dios, grande y pacífico Emperador ». El Vaticano, y Roma con ello, ya volvíase así la expresión de una nueva dominación universal: la del Santo Imperio.

Los beneficios de este gran acontecimiento, extendidos gradualmente a todo el mundo cristiano, afirmáronse especialmente en Roma y en el Vaticano, donde el poder guerrero de los Cesares fué reemplazado por la potencia pacífica de los Papas, quienes asumieron una autoridad y un prestigio de que la soberanía temporal fué tan solo, y por pocos siglos, un palido reflejo. Pero aquel movimiento volvióse también una solicitación poderosa a la unión de las naciones para la paz, bajo la tutela de los poderes fundamentales de la sociedad, la Iglesia y el Estado. Y a pesar de el ideal soñado entonces nunca haber sido enteramente alcanzando, no dejo de acarrear, aún entre contrastes innumerables, beneficios incalculables. Por la primera vez comprendióse que las naciones cristianas, aún divididas por razas, lenguas e instituciones sociales, habian que formar familia única, y colaborar para los intereses comunes de la civilización. Fué así posible, con el tiempo, resolver la lucha para las « investiduras », emprender las cruzadas que pusieron en contacto a los Europeos y los Asiáticos, y promover aquel movimiento jurídico, filosófico y literario de donde nacieron el *Decretum* de Graciano, la Suma Teologica de S. Tomas, la Comedia de Dante, y, junto con ellos, el renacimiento de las artes y de las ciencias de que fué alimentado la civilización moderna.

Es fácil pués explicarse como y porque al Vaticano se volviesen los admiradores del mundo clásico juntos con los cultores de las más antiguas memorias cristianas, los romeros, los representantes más distinguidos de las artes y de la sabeduría de todo el mundo, y con ellos llegasen al Vaticano presentes preciosos destinados a enriquecer los monumentos y atestiguar la veneración y la afición de todos los creyentes. En este movimiento, que continuó de siglo en siglo hasta nuestros dias, hallan su orígen los tesoros de arte de la Basílica y del Palacio Vaticano, conocidos en todo el mundo civil, especialmente los de la Basílica del Príncipe de los Apóstoles. Iniciada por Constantino en 324 y cumplida en 349, la Basílica debía aunar en si todas las expresiones artísticas más fúlgidas del suntuoso periodo final del Imperio Romano. Los históricos del tiempo y el *Liber Pontificalis* dán noticias asombrosas de aquellos tesoros; pero de las antiguas riquezas de la era de Constantino y de las de los siglos siguientes muy poco escapó a las destrucciones y a los saqueos. Entre los monumentos que llegaron hasta nuestros dias podemos mencionar: la cruz de plata dorada esparcida de gemas, dádiva de Justin II Emperador de Constantinopla y de Sofia su consorte (570) que contiene un pedazo de la Cruz de Jesucristo; la así llamada dalmática de Carlomagno, obra de arte bizantina del siglo XIV importada de Constantinopla después de la destrucción de aquella ciudad (1433); una estátua antigua de filósofo transformada en estátua de San Pedro, antaño colocada en el atrio y ahora en las Grutas, o la otra estátua de bronce venerada en la Basílica; los mosaicos de la Capilla de Juan VII (705-707); las tumbas de Otón III (983) y de Bonifacio VIII (1294-1305), esta última atribuida a Arnolfo de Cambio; el políptico encomendado a Giotto por el Cardenal Stefaneschi (cerca de 1300) para el Altar de la Confesión, que hállase ahora en la Pinacoteca Vaticana. Había siempre quedado de pié la Basílica en su estructura original; pero los seismos, el descuido de los hombres y, aún más, la acción deletérea del tiempo la habían reducido en condicciones tán peligrosas que, hácia le mitad del siglo XV, Nicolas V (1447-1455) había resolvido su reconstrucción.

La muerte del Pontífice causó la interrupción de las obras, que quedaron suspendidas por cincuenta años, hasta que Julio II (1503-1513) confió la ejecución de los trabajos a Bramante: en 1506 fué puesta la primera piedra. Más una vez, pero, la muerte, pocos años más tarde, del Pontífice (1513) y del arquitecto (1514) lentificó a la ejecución de los trabajos. Intencionado a truncar los retrasos, Pablo III en 1546 confió las obras a Miguel Ángel, dejándole las más amplias facultades de ensanchar, empequeñecer o transformar todo conforme su proprio juicio. Y Miguel Ángel, a pesar de sus setenta y dos años, renunciando, con elevado espíritu religioso, a toda retribución, aceptó el encargo. Retomo él el dibujo de Bramante que había proyectado un templo de cruz griega, pero a la cúpula del Pantheon imaginada por Bramante la reemplazó con otra cúpula poco menos ancha pero muy más alta, inspirándose a la de Brunelleschi en Florencia; y para dar a sus succesores una guía segura en la continuación de la obra, mando él hacer bajo sus dibujos un modelo de madera, que todavía hace parte de los objetos más raros de la Fábrica de San Pedro. Arrebatado por la muerte en 1564, Miguel Ángel no pudo ver la terminación de los trabajos; esta dicha les tocó a Doménico Fontana y a Giácomo della Porta que, con unas pequeñas modificaciones, dieron el remate a la obra (1590). Desde hace aquel dia a las siete colinas de Roma se les añadió más una, más grande y majestuosa, que domina a las amplias soledades de Lacio hasta las últimas estribaciones de la Sabina, meta anhelada por todos los romeros del arte y de la fe, que reconocen en ella un símbolo de unidad, de paz y de esperanzas que desde las miserias de la tierra se levantan hácia la visión del cielo. El monumento habría sido más perfecto como Miguel Ángel lo había proyectado, bajo el punto de vista artístico: pero las necesidades del culto aconsejaron de añadir un arimez que, aumentando a la capacidad del templo, le dió la forma de cruz latina. El alargamiento, el pórtico y la fachada fueron acabados por el arquitecto Maderno en 1614; en el periodo de 1656 a 1666, Lorenzo Bernini completó a la obra colosal con los brazos laterales del pórtico y de la columnata de la plaza. Las grandes estátuas ecuestres de Constantino y de Carlomagno a las extremidades de los brazos laterales, donde estos se encuentran con el pórtico de la Basílica, eran las centinelas a la guarda, mientras que las 140 estátuas de Mártires y Confesores de la Fe colocadas encima de los cornisones de los brazos y de la columnata eran el coro que habría cantado perennemente el himno de gloria al Príncipe de los Apóstoles. Tuvo así su forma final un conjunto arquitectónico único en el mundo, que «durará como el mundo lejano» (Dante, *Infierno*, II, 60; véase pág. 33).

Pasando al interior de la Basílica, quedamos impresionados por la grandiosidad de las líneas que no nos permiten percibir a toda la preciosidad y la infinita variedad de los pormenores (pág. 38). Será menester detenernos aquí tán solo sobre los principales. El altar de la Confesión, dominado por el pabellón de Bernini, inaugurado por Urbano VIII en 1633, y por la cúpula de Miguel Ángel (págs. 35, 36, 40); detrás de la Confesión, el Altar de la Cátedra, obra esta también de Bernini (1658-1666) que, con la Cátedra misma, con las estátuas colosales de los Doctores de la Iglesia que la sostienen, con la mística paloma en la vidriera que la ilumina, con una miríada de angelitos que le hacen corona, injértase armonicamente en la arquitectura y expresa en una síntesis maravillosa a las orígenes y a las funciones de la Iglesia Católica (págs. 41-43).

Además de estos altares, que son los centros máximos de la Basilica, hay dos altares más que merecen nuestra atención: él de la Piedad, así llamado por el grupo marmóreo (1498) donde Miguel Ángel supo transfundir a su fe en el misterio de la Redención (págs. 44-46), y él del Santísimo Sacramento, donde domina, entre dos angeles arrodillados, un sagrario de bronce dorado, obra de Bernini (1674-1675) que recuerda a las formas del templito de Bramante sobre el Janículo. Junto con los demás hacen ornamento a la Basílica los monumentos honorarios y sepulcrales, que prodrían servirnos para marcar a los fundamentos de la escultura desde el Renacimiento hasta nuestros dias: los monumentos de Pablo III por Guglielmo Della Porta (págs. 47, 48), de Urbano VIII por Bernini (pág. 49), de Clemente XIII y de Pio VI por Canova. Un segundo monumento, dedicado a Pio VI, hállase a la extremidad de la escalera de la Sacristía, obra de inspiración barroca pero de efecto muy bueno, moldeada por Gáspare Sibilia y ejecutada por Agostino Penna a fines del 1700 (pág. 51). Un cumplemento necesario de la Basílica son el Tesoro anexo a la Sacristía y las Grutas, nombre con que indicase la parte subterránea de la Basílica Constantiniana, preservada en las tres naves centrales y en la Confesión que custodia a las reliquias del Príncipe de los Apóstoles.

En el Tesoro hállanse la Cruz del Emperador Justín y la dalmática de Carlomagno, ya mencionadas arriba, además de muchas obras de orfebrería y de cincel que constituyen atestaciones fundamentales de estas artes desde la Edad Media hasta nuestros dias. En las Grutas, además de la estátua de San Pedro en Cátedra, de los mosaicos y de las tumbas ya mencionadas de Otón y de Bonifacio VIII, llaman a nuestra atención el monumento sepulcral de Sixto IV (1471-1484) por Pollaiolo, que es considerado la obra en bronce más perfecta del Renacimiento italiano; además los bajorrelieves y las esculturas de Mino de Fiésole y de Giovanni Dálmata, que constituían la parte principal de la tumba de Pablo II (1464-1471), descompuesta cuando fué derribada la vieja basílica.

Ainsi que nous l'avons dit tout d'abord, dans l'immense bouleversement qui accompagna la chute de l'Empire Romain et durant lequel les trésors accumulés par la civilisation classique furent pour la plupart dispersés et détruits, la Basilique vaticane seule survécut, réparant bien vite les pertes subies et devenant à nouveau le centre d'attraction de tous les peuples. Un petit nombre d'années s'étaient écoulées depuis les incursions des Goths, commandés par Alaric (410) et des Vandales, conduits par Genséric (455) que déjà l'on voyait d'autres flots de barbares accourir du septentrion par les vieilles voies consulaires; mais ils ne portaient point d'armes, ne poussaient pas des cris de guerre et ne méditaient pas carnages, incendies et ruines: ils arboraient la croix et psalmodiaient des chants religieux. Ils venaient s'agenouiller au pied d'un autel, devant un vieux prêtre pour lui demander sa bénédiction; ils s'étaient dépouillés de leurs richesses pour les déposer sur le tombeau du Prince des Apôtres. Et c'est ainsi que de nouvelles foules d'Angles, de Francs, de Saxons, de Frisons, héritiers des anciens envahisseurs, retournèrent à Rome comme à la mère des nations, et le temple vatican n'eut dès lors plus rien à envier au Capitole exalté par Horace, paré de ses armes conquises, éclatant de tous les ors rassemblés du fond des plus lointaines provinces. Et de Rome partirent, envoyés par Grégoire le Grand, des légions de moines guidés par saint Boniface vers l'Allemagne, et par saint Augustin vers l'Angleterre, et ces moines allaient compenser les pertes subies par la poussée menaçante du Croissant, acquérir à l'Eglise de nouvelles foules de fidèles et leur confier le soin de garder dans les codes ce qui avait été légué en héritage par la civilisation classique. Deux siècles encore et dans la Basilique Vaticane, durant la nuit de Noël de l'an 800, Charles, roi des Francs, sera couronné empereur parmi les acclamations du peuple: « A Carlo piissimo, augusto, coronato da Dio, grande e pacifico imperatore ». Le Vatican, et Rome par lui, devenait le siège d'une nouvelle domination universelle, du Saint Empire Romain.

Les avantages de ce grand événement, peu à peu élargis au monde chrétien tout entier, s'affirmèrent, comme il est naturel, notamment à Rome et au Vatican. A la puissance guerrière des Césars succéda celle toute pacifique des Papes qui acquirent une autorité et un prestige dont le pouvoir temporel ne fut guère, et pour quelques siècles, qu'un pâle reflet. Mais ce mouvement devint néanmoins un puissant appel à l'union des nations pour la paix sous la tutelle des pouvoirs fondamentaux de la société, l'Eglise et l'Etat. Si cet idéal entrevu ce jour là ne fut jamais atteint, en dépit de toutes les dissensions il n'en produisit pas moins des bénéfices incalculables. Pour la première fois peut-être on comprit alors que les nations chrétiennes, quoique séparées par la race, la langue et les institutions sociales, étaient appelées à former une seule famille et à collaborer en vue des intérêts communs de la civilisation. Par la suite des temps, il fut possible dès lors de résoudre la querelle des investitures, de prêcher les croisades qui rouvraient l'Orient à l'Occident, et de promouvoir ce mouvement juridique, philosophique, théologique et littéraire d'où découlèrent et par où prirent forme le *Decretum* de Gratien, la Somme Théologique de saint Thomas, la Divine Comédie de Dante, et avec eux la renaissance des arts et des sciences dont s'est nourrie la civilisation moderne. Il est donc facile de s'expliquer comment et pourquoi vers le Vatican, Basilique et Siège Pontifical, se tournèrent à la fois les admirateurs du monde classique, les fervents des plus antiques souvenirs chrétiens, les pèlerins, les représentants les plus remarquables des arts et du savoir, et affluèrent avec eux les dons précieux destinés à enrichir les monuments, à témoigner du respect et de l'affection de tous les croyants. C'est de ce mouvement, qui s'est propagé de siècle en siècle jusqu'à nos jours, que tirent aussi leur origine les trésors d'art, ceux de la Basilique et ceux du Palais du Vatican, dont la renommée retentit dans le monde civilisé; tout d'abord ceux de la Basilique du Prince des Apôtres.

Commencée par Constantin en 324 et achevée en 349, la Basilique devait rassembler ce que les arts pouvaient offrir de mieux, dans le somptueux déclin de l'Empire Romain. Les historiens du temps et le *Liber Pontificalis* en donnent des échos stupéfiants, mais des antiques richesses de l'ère constantinienne et de celles qui les ont remplacées dans les siècles suivants bien peu de chose a échappé aux pillages et à la destruction. Parmi les monuments qui subsistent on peut citer: la croix d'argent doré constellée de pierreries, don de Justinien II empereur de Constantinople et de son épouse Sophie (570), qui contient un morceau de la vraie croix, et la dalmatique dite de Charlemagne, ouvrage d'art byzantin du XIVe siècle rapporté de Constantinople après la destruction de la ville (1453); une statue antique de philosophe transformée en celle de saint Pierre, jadis dans l'atrium et aujourd'hui conservée dans les cryptes, et l'autre statue de bronze vénérée dans la Basilique; les mosaïques de la chapelle de Jean VII (705-707); les tombeaux d'Othon III (983) et de Boniface VIII (1294-1305), ce dernier attribué à Arnolfo di Cambio, le polyptyque de Giotto du Cardinal Stefaneschi (vers 1300) pour l'autel de

26

la Confession aujourd'hui dans la Pinacothèque du Vatican. La Basilique, elle, était restée debout dans sa structure originaire; mais les tremblements de terre, l'incurie des hommes et plus encore l'action délétère du temps l'avaient réduite en des conditions si périlleuses que, vers le milieu du XVe siècle, Nicolas V (1447-1453) en avait décidé la reconstruction. La mort du Pontife interrompit les travaux à peine commencés et cinquante années passèrent dans l'inactivité, jusqu'à ce que Jules II (1503-1513) reprenant l'idée en confia l'exécution à Bramante, et en 1506 fut posée la première pierre. Mais la mort du Pontife à quelques années de là (1513), et de l'architecte (1514) ralentit cette fois-ci encore les travaux. Résolu à les poursuivre sans délai, Paul III en 1546 recourut à Michel-Ange, lui laissant la plus large faculté d'agrandir, de rapetisser ou de transformer le tout comme bon lui semblerait. Et Michel-Ange, malgré ses soixante-douze ans, renonçant par un sentiment profond de religiosité à toute compensation, accepta la tâche. Il reprit de Bramante le dessin d'une église en croix-grecque, mais à la coupole du Panthéon imaginée par Bramante il en substitua une autre, inférieure de peu en largeur, mais beaucoup plus élevée en hauteur, inspirée par celle de Brunelleschi à Florence et, pour que ses successeurs eussent un guide sûr dans la continuation de l'ouvrage, il en fit exécuter sous ses yeux un modèle en bois que l'on conserve encore aujourd'hui parmi les objets les plus rares de la Fabrique de Saint-Pierre. Emporté par la mort en 1564, Michel-Ange ne put voir l'achèvement de son œuvre. Ce bonheur échut en revanche à Domenico Fontana et à Giacomo della Porta, qui avec de légères modifications purent achever la coupole (1590). A partir de ce jour, aux sept collines de Rome il s'en adjoignit une autre bien plus grande et bien plus majestueuse, qui domine sans conteste sur les vastes solitudes du Latium jusqu'aux dernières ramifications de la Sabine, terme désiré de tous les pèlerins de l'art et de la foi, car ils voient en elle un symbole d'unité, de paix et d'espérance qui les élève des lieux bas de la terre à la vision du ciel.

Un monument tel que l'avait projeté Michel-Ange aurait été d'un art plus parfait; mais les nécessités du culte conseillèrent d'y adjoindre un avant-corps qui, tout en augmentant les dimensions de l'église, lui donna la forme d'une croix-latine. La rallonge, le portique et la façade furent terminés par l'architecte Maderno en 1614. Bernini, dans les années de 1656 à 1666, couronna cette œuvre colossale par les ailes latérales du portique et de la colonnade de la place. Les grandes statues équestres de Constantin et de Charlemagne aux extrémités des ailes latérales, où ils se recontrent avec le portique de la Basilique, étaient les sentinelles montant la garde. Les cent-quarante statues de Martyrs et de Confesseurs de la Foi rangées sur les corniches des ailes et de la colonnade étaient le chœur qui devait chanter perpétuellement l'hymne de gloire au Prince des Apôtres. Un ensemble architectural unique au monde reçut ainsi sa forme définitive, ensemble qui « durerà quanto il mondo lontano » (Dante, *Inferno*, II, 60; voir à page 33).

Si de l'extérieur on passe à l'intérieur de la Basilique, l'œil reste frappé de la grandiose disposition des lignes qui ne permettent pas de saisir du premier coup la préciosité et la variété infinie des détails (page 38). Nous devons ici nous borner à indiquer les principaux. L'autel de la Confession, que surmontent le Baldaquin du Bernini, inauguré par Urbain VIII en 1633, et la coupole de Michel-Ange (pages 35, 36, 40); au-delà de la Confession, l'autel de la Chaire, œuvre elle aussi de Bernini (1658-1666), qui avec la Chaire elle même, avec les figures colossales des Docteurs de l'Eglise qui la soutiennent et la Colombe mystique du vitrail en haut qui l'éclaire, avec une nuée d'angelots qui forment autour d'elle une couronne, est harmonieusement greffée sur l'architecture pour exprimer dans une synthèse merveilleuse les origines et les fonctions de l'Eglise catholique (pages 41-43). Après ces autels, qui sont les centres principaux de la Basilique, deux autres méritent d'être remarqués: celui de la Pietà, dite ainsi d'après le groupe en marbre dans lequel Michel-Ange (1498) a transfusé l'intensité de sa foi au mystère de la Rédemption (pages 44-46), et celui du Très Saint-Sacrement sur lequel trône, entre deux anges à genoux, un tabernacle en bronze doré, œuvre du Bernini (1674-1675), qui rappelle les formes du petit temple de Bramante au Janicule. La Basilique, outre les autels, a pour ornements les monuments commémoratifs et sépulcraux qui pourraient être des points de repère de la sculpture de la Renaissance jusqu'à notre époque: les monuments de Paul III par Guglielmo Della Porta (pages 47, 48), d'Urbain VIII par Bernini (page 49), de Clément XIII et de Pie VI par Canova. Un second monument dédié à Pie VI est au commencement de l'escalier de l'entrée de la sacristie, œuvre d'inspiration baroque, mais d'un grand effet, modelée par Gaspard Sibilia et exécutée par Agostino Penna sur la fin du XVIe siècle (page 51). La Basilique a pour complément nécessaire le Trésor annexé à la Sacristie et les Grottes, nom sous lequel on désigne la partie souterraine de la Basilique constantinienne conservée dans ses trois nefs centrales et dans la Confession qui garde les reliques du Prince des Apôtres. Il y a dans le Trésor la croix de l'empereur Justin et la dalmatique de Charlemagne, citées plus haut, et de nombreux ouvrages d'orfèvrerie et de ciselure qui rendent témoignage de ces arts du Moyen âge jusqu'à nos jours. Dans les Grottes, outre la statue de saint Pierre en chaire, les mosaïques et les tombeaux déjà cités d'Othon et de Boniface VIII, notre attention est appelée par le monument sépulcral de Sixte IV (1471-1484) du Pollaiolo, considéré comme l'ouvrage en bronze le plus parfait de la Renaissance italienne; en outre par les bas-reliefs et les sculptures de Mino da Fiesole et de Giovanni Dalmata, qui formaient la partie principale du tombeau de Paul II (1464-1471) démonté lorsque l'ancienne basilique fut démolie.

Come fu detto già da principio, nell'immane sconvolgimento che accompagnò la caduta dell'Impero Romano e nel quale i tesori accumulati dalla civiltà classica andarono per la massima parte dispersi o distrutti, soltanto la basilica Vaticana sopravvisse, riparando celermente le perdite subite e diventando nuovo centro di attrazione per tutti i popoli. Non erano trascorsi molti anni dalle incursioni dei Goti, capitanati da Alarico (410), e dei Vandali, condotti da Genserico (455), quando altre schiere di barbari si videro arrivare da settentrione per le vecchie vie consolari; ma essi non portavano armi, non intonavano canzoni di guerra, non meditavano stragi, incendi e rovine: levavano alto le croci e cantavano salmodie religiose. Essi venivano per inginocchiarsi ai piedi di un altare, dinanzi ad un vecchio sacerdote, a cui chiedere una benedizione; si erano spogliati delle loro ricchezze per deporle sulla tomba del Principe degli Apostoli. E così avvenne che nuove schiere di Angli, di Franchi, di Sassoni, di Frisoni, eredi degli antichi invasori, tornassero a Roma, come alla madre venerata delle genti; e il tempio Vaticano nulla ebbe più da invidiare al Campidoglio esaltato da Orazio, superbo di armi conquistate, fulgente di marmi e di ori radunati dalle lontane province. E da Roma, mandati da Gregorio Magno, partirono legioni di monaci, guidati da S. Bonifacio per la Germania e da S. Agostino per l'Inghilterra, i quali, a compensare le perdite subite per l'avanzarsi minaccioso della Mezzaluna, acquisteranno qui alla Chiesa nuove turbe di fedeli e affideranno a loro da custodire nei codici quanto di meglio aveva lasciato in eredità la civiltà classica. Due secoli ancora, e nella Basilica Vaticana, nella notte di Natale dell' 800, Carlo, re dei Franchi, sarà coronato imperatore fra le acclamazioni del popolo « a Carlo piissimo augusto, coronato da Dio, grande e pacifico imperatore ». Il Vaticano, e Roma per esso, diventava sede di una nuova dominazione universale, del Sacro Romano Impero.

I benefici di questo grande avvenimento, estesi gradatamente a tutto il mondo cristiano, si affermarono, com'è naturale, specialmente in Roma e nel Vaticano, dove alla potenza guerriera dei Cesari subentrò quella pacifica dei Papi, i quali assunsero un'autorità ed un prestigio, di cui il dominio temporale fu soltanto, e per pochi secoli, un pallido riflesso. Ma quel movimento diventò pure un poderoso appello all'unione delle nazioni per la pace, sotto la tutela dei poteri fondamentali della società, la Chiesa e lo Stato. Che se l'ideale vagheggiato in quel giorno non fu mai interamente raggiunto, pur tra innumerevoli contrasti, produsse benefici incalcolabili. Per la prima volta, forse, si comprese che le nazioni cristiane, benchè divise di razza, di lingua e di istituzioni sociali, erano chiamate a formare una sola famiglia, e a collaborare per gli interessi comuni della civiltà. Quindi fu possibile, con l'andare dei tempi, risolvere la lotta per le « investiture », bandire le crociate che riaprirono l'Oriente all'Occidente, e promuovere quel movimento giuridico, filosofico, e letterario dal quale e per il quale scaturirono il *Decretum* di Graziano, la Somma Teologica di S. Tommaso, la Commedia di Dante, e insieme con essi la rinascita delle arti e delle scienze di cui si è nutrita la civiltà moderna. È facile quindi spiegarsi come e perchè al Vaticano, Basilica e sede Pontificia, si volgessero insieme gli ammiratori del mondo classico, i cultori delle più antiche memorie cristiane, i pellegrini, i rappresentanti più insigni delle arti e del sapere, e con loro affluissero doni preziosi destinati ad arricchire i monumenti, a testimoniare la riverenza e l'affetto di tutti i credenti. Da questo movimento, che si è prorogato di secolo in secolo fino ai nostri giorni, traggono origine anche i tesori d'arte tanto della Basilica quanto del Palazzo Vaticano, di cui risuona la fama nel mondo civile; innanzi tutto della Basilica del Principe degli Apostoli. Iniziata da Costantino nel 324 e compiuta nel 349, essa doveva adunare in sè quanto di meglio potevano offrire le arti nel lussuoso tramonto dell'impero romano. Gli storici del tempo e il *Liber Pontificalis* ne danno strabilianti notizie; ma delle antiche ricchezze dell'era costantiniana e di quelle rinnovatesi nei secoli posteriori ben poco si è salvato dalle distruzioni e dalle rapine. Fra i monumenti rimasti si possono citare: la croce d'argento dorato tempestata di gemme, dono di Giustino II imperatore di Costantinopoli e di Sofia sua moglie (570), che contiene un pezzo della vera croce; e la cosidetta dalmatica di Carlo Magno, opera d'arte bizantina del secolo XIV, importata da Costantinopoli dopo la distruzione di quella città (1453); una statua antica di filosofo trasformata in quella di S. Pietro, una volta nell'atrio ed ora custodita nelle Grotte, o l'altra statua di bronzo venerata nella Basilica; i mosaici della Cappella di Giovanni VII (705-707); le tombe di Ottone III (983) e quella di Bonifacio VIII (1294-1305) attribuita ad Arnolfo di Cambio, il politico di Giotto fatto dipingere dal Cardinale Stefaneschi (circa il 1300) per l'altare della Confessione ed ora nella Pinacoteca Vaticana. Era rimasta sempre in piedi la Basilica nella sua originaria struttura; ma i terremoti, l'incuria degli uomini e più ancora l'azione deleteria del tempo l'avevano ridotta in condizioni così pericolose, che alla metà del secolo XV Niccolò V (1447-1455) ne aveva deliberato la ricostruzione.

La morte del Pontefice interruppe i lavori appena incominciati e passarono cinquant'anni inoperosi; fino a che Giulio II (1503-1513), riprendendo l'idea, ne affidò l'esecuzione a Bramante e nel 1506 fu posta la prima pietra. Ma ancora una volta la morte avvenuta pochi anni dopo del Pontefice (1513) e dell'architetto (1514), rallentò i lavori. Deciso a troncare gli indugi Paolo III ricorse (1546) a Michelangelo, lasciandogli le più ampie facoltà di ampliare, restringere o trasformare tutto a suo giudizio. E Michelangelo, non ostante i suoi settantadue anni, rinunciando con alto senso di religiosità a qualsiasi compenso accettò l'incarico. Riprese da Bramante il disegno di un tempio a croce greca, ma alla cupola del Pantheon immaginata da Bramante ne sostituì un'altra di poco inferiore in larghezza, di gran lunga più elevata in altezza, ispirata da quella del Brunelleschi a Firenze; e perchè i suoi successori avessero una guida sicura nella continuazione dell'opera, ne fece eseguire sotto i suoi occhi un modello in legno, che si conserva tuttora fra i cimeli più rari della Fabbrica di S. Pietro. Rapito dalla morte nel 1564, Michelangelo non potè vedere la fine dell'opera. Questa fortuna toccò invece a Domenico Fontana e a Giacomo della Porta, i quali con lievi modifiche portarono la cupola a compimento (1590). Da quel giorno ai sette colli di Roma se ne aggiunse un altro ben più grande e maestoso, che domina incontrastato sulle vaste solitudini del Lazio fino alle ultime propaggini della Sabina, meta agognata di tutti i pellegrini dell'arte e della fede, che ravvisano in essa un simbolo di unità, di pace e di speranze che dalle bassure della terra si innalzano alla visione del cielo.

Un monumento, quale Michelangelo lo aveva progettato, sarebbe stato artisticamente il più perfetto; ma le necessità del culto consigliarono l'aggiunta di un avancorpo, che, aumentando le capacità del tempio, gli diede la forma di croce latina. Il prolungamento, il portico e la facciata furono terminati dall'architetto Maderno nel 1614: Lorenzo Bernini negli anni 1656-1666 coronò l'opera colossale coi bracci laterali del portico e del colonnato della piazza. Le grandi statue equestri di Costantino e di Carlo Magno alle estremità dei bracci laterali, dove essi s'incontrano col portico della Basilica, erano le sentinelle di guardia. Le centoquaranta statue di Martiri e Confessori della Fede schierate sui cornicioni dei bracci e del colonnato erano il coro che avrebbe cantato perennemente l'inno di gloria al Principe degli Apostoli. Così ebbe la sua forma definitiva un complesso architettonico unico al mondo, e che « durerà quanto il mondo lontano » (Dante, *Inferno*, II, 60; vedi pag. 33).

Che se dall'esterno si passa all'interno della Basilica, l'occhio rimane colpito dalla grandiosità delle linee che non lasciano afferrare a tutta prima la preziosità e l'infinita varietà dei particolari (pag. 38). Bisognerà soffermarsi qui soltanto sui principali: l'altare della Confessione, a cui sovrastano il baldacchino del Bernini, inaugurato da Urbano VIII nel 1633, e la cupola di Michelangelo (pagg. 35, 36, 40); al di là della Confessione, l'altare della Cattedra, opera essa pure del Bernini (1658-1666), che con la Cattedra stessa, con le figure colossali dei dottori della Chiesa che la sorreggono, con la mistica colomba in alto nella vetrata che la illumina, con una miriade di angioletti che le fanno corona, s'innesta armonicamente nell'architettura ed esprime in sintesi meravigliosa le origini e le funzioni della Chiesa Cattolica (pagg. 41-43).

Dopo questi altari che sono i centri massimi della Basilica, due altri meritano di essere considerati: quello della Pietà, detta così dal gruppo marmoreo nel quale Michelangelo (1498) ha trasfuso l'intensità della sua fede nel mistero della Redenzione (pagg. 44-46) e quello del SS. Sacramento, su cui troneggia, fra due angeli genuflessi, un tabernacolo di bronzo dorato, opera del Bernini (1674-1675), che richeggia le forme del tempietto di Bramante al Gianicolo. Insieme con gli altari fanno ornamento alla Basilica i monumenti onorari e sepolcrali, coi quali si potrebbero segnare i capisaldi della scultura dal Rinascimento fino ai giorni nostri: i monumenti di Paolo III di Guglielmo Della Porta (pagg. 47, 48), di Urbano VIII del Bernini (pag. 49), di Clemente XIII e di Pio VI del Canova. Un secondo monumento dedicato a Pio VI è a capo della scala della Sagrestia, opera d'ispirazione barocca, ma di buon effetto, modellata da Gaspare Sibilia ed eseguita da Agostino Penna sulla fine del '700 (pag. 51). Necessario complemento della Basilica sono il Tesoro annesso alla Sagrestia e le Grotte, col qual nome si designa la parte sotterranea della Basilica Costantiniana conservata nelle tre navate centrali e nella Confessione che custodisce le reliquie del Principe degli Apostoli.

Nel Tesoro sono la croce dell'Imperatore Giustino e la dalmatica di Carlo Magno, già citate sopra, e molte opere di oreficeria e di cesello che fanno testimonio di queste arti del Medio-Evo fino ai giorni nostri. Nelle Grotte, oltre la statua di S. Pietro in Cattedra, i mosaici e le tombe già citate di Ottone e Bonifacio VIII, richiamano l'attenzione il monumento sepolcrale di Sisto IV (1471-1484), del Pollaiolo, considerato come l'opera più perfetta in bronzo del Rinascimento italiano; inoltre i bassorilievi e le sculture di Mino da Fiesole e di Giovanni Dalmata, che formavano la parte principale della tomba di Paolo II (1464-1471), scomposta quando fu demolita la vecchia basilica.

Façade of the Basilica - Fachada de la Basílica
Façade de la Basilique - Facciata della Basilica

St. Peter's Square - Plaza San Pedro
Place Saint-Pierre - Piazza S. Pietro

33

Colonnades of Bernini - Columnada de Bernini
Colonnade de Bernini - Colonnato del Bernini

Dome of St. Peter (exterior) - Cúpula de San Pedro (exterior)
Coupole de Saint-Pierre (extérieur) - Cupola di S. Pietro (esterno)

Dome of St. Peter (interior) - Cúpula de San Pedro (interior)
Coupole de Saint-Pierre (intérieur) - Cupola di S. Pietro (interno)

L. Bernini: *Equestrian Statue of Constantine* - L. Bernini: *Estátua ecuestre de Constantino*
L. Bernini: *Statue de Constantin à cheval* - L. Bernini: *Statua equestre di Costantino*

C. Maderno: *Atrium of the Basilica* - C. Maderno: *Atrio de la Basílica*
C. Maderno: *Porche de la Basilique* - C. Maderno: *Atrio della Basilica*

Principal Nave of the Basilica - Nave principal de la Basílica
Nef centrale de la Basilique - Navata principale della Basilica

Bronze Statue of St. Peter - Estátua de bronce de San Pedro
Statue en bronze de saint Pierre - Statua in bronzo di S. Pietro

Baldacchino and Papal Altar - Pabellón y Altar de la Confesión
Baldaquin et Autel de la Confession - Baldacchino e Altare della Confessione

40

Altar of the cathedra Petri - Altar de la Cátedra
Autel de la Chaire - Altare della Cattedra

Altar of the Cathedra Petri (detail) - Altar de la Cátedra (detalle)
Autel de la Chaire (détail) - Altare della Cattedra (particolare)

Altar of the Cathedra Petri (detail) - Altar de la Cátedra (detalle)
Autel de la Chaire (détail) - Altare della Cattedra (particolare)

Michelangelo: *Pietà* - Miguel Ángel: *La Piedad*
Michel-Ange: *La Pietà* - Michelangelo: *La Pietà*

Michelangelo: *Pietà* (detail) - Miguel Ángel: *La Piedad* (detalle)
Michel-Ange: *La Pietà* (détail) - Michelangelo: *La Pietà* (particolare)

Michelangelo: *Pietà* (detail) - Miguel Angel: *La Piedad* (detalle)
Michel-Ange: *La Pietà* (détail) - Michelangelo: *La Pietà* (particolare)

46

Guglielmo Della Porta: *Monument of Paul III* (the Pope)
Guglielmo Della Porta: *Monumento de Pablo III* (el Papa)
Guglielmo Della Porta: *Monument de Paul III* (le Pape)
Guglielmo Della Porta: *Monumento di Paolo III* (il Papa)

Guglielmo Della Porta: *Monument of Paul III* (Justice, detail)
Guglielmo Della Porta: *Monumento de Pablo III* (la Justicia, detalle)
Guglielmo Della Porta: *Monument de Paul III* (la Justice, détail)
Guglielmo Della Porta: *Monumento di Paolo III* (la Giustizia, particolare)

L. Bernini: *Monument of Urban VIII* - L. Bernini: *Monumento de Urbano VIII*
L. Bernini: *Monument d'Urbain VIII* - L. Bernini: *Monumento di Urbano VIII*

Antonio Canova: *Monument of Clement XIII* (detail) - Antonio Canova: *Monumento de Clemente XIII* (detalle)
Antonio Canova: *Monument de Clément XIII* (détail) - Antonio Canova: *Monumento di Clemente XIII* (particolare)

Gaspare Sibilia: *Monument of Pius VI* - Gáspare Sibilia: *Monumento de Pio VI*
Gaspare Sibilia: *Monument de Pie VI* - Gaspare Sibilia: *Monumento di Pio VI*

51

Cross of the Emperor Justin (Treasure) - Cruz del Emperador Justin (Tesoro)
Croix de l'Empereur Justin (Trésor) - Croce dell'Imperatore Giustino (Tesoro)

Castellani: *Cover of a XIX century Gospel Book* (Treasure)
Castellani: *Cubierta de Evangeliario del siglo XIX* (Tesoro)
Castellani: *Couverture de l'Evangéliaire, XIXᵉ siècle* (Trésor)
Castellani: *Copertura di Evangeliario del sec. XIX* (Tesoro)

53

Dalmatica of Charlemagne (detail, Treasure) - Dalmática de Carlomagno (detalle, Tesoro)
Dalmatique de Charlemagne (détail, Trésor) - Dalmatica di Carlo Magno (particolare, Tesoro)

Marble Statue of St. Peter (Grottoes) - Estátua marmórea de San Pedro (Grutas)
Statue en marbre de saint Pierre (Grottes) - Statua marmorea di S. Pietro (Grotte)

A. Pollaiolo: *Monument of Sixtus IV* - A. Pollaiolo: *Monumento de Sixto IV*
A. Pollaiolo: *Monument de Sixte IV* - A. Pollaiolo: *Monumento di Sisto IV*

A. Pollaiolo: *Monument of Sixtus IV* (detail) - A. Pollaiolo: *Monumento de Sixto IV* (detalle)
A. Pollaiolo: *Monument de Sixte IV* (détail) - A. Pollaiolo: *Monumento di Sisto IV* (particolare)

A. Pollaiolo: *Monument of Sixtus IV* (detail) - A. Pollaiolo: *Monumento de Sixto IV* (detalle)
A. Pollaiolo: *Monument de Sixte IV* (détail) - A. Pollaiolo: *Monumento di Sisto IV* (particolare)

Mino da Fiesole and Giovanni Dalmata: *Monument of Paul II* (detail)
Mino da Fiesole y Giovanni Dalmata: *Monumento de Pablo II* (detalle)
Mino da Fiesole et Giovanni Dalmata: *Monument de Paul II* (détail)
Mino da Fiesole e Giovanni Dalmata: *Monumento di Paolo II* (particolare)

Mino da Fiesole and Giovanni Dalmata: *Monument of Paul II* (detail)
Mino da Fiesole y Giovanni Dalmata: *Monumento de Pablo II* (detalle)
Mino da Fiesole et Giovanni Dalmata: *Monument de Paul II* (détail)
Mino da Fiesole e Giovanni Dalmata: *Monumento di Paolo II* (particolare)

Mino da Fiesole and Giovanni Dalmata: *Monument of Paul II* (detail)
Mino da Fiesole y Giovanni Dalmata: *Monumento de Pablo II* (detalle)
Mino da Fiesole et Giovanni Dalmata: *Monument de Paul II* (détail)
Mino da Fiesole e Giovanni Dalmata: *Monumento di Paolo II* (particolare)

Arnolfo: *Bust of Boniface VIII* (Grottoes) - Arnolfo: *Busto de Bonifacio VIII* (Grutas)
Arnolfo: *Buste de Boniface VIII* (Grottes) - Arnolfo: *Busto di Bonifacio VIII* (Grotte)

THE  PALACE

EL  PALACIO

LE  PALAIS

IL  PALAZZO

Belvedere Court from the South side - Patio del Belvedere (lado sul)
Cour du Belvédère du côté sud - Cortile del Belvedere dal lato Sud

The Vatican Palace is composed of a group of buildings which sum up the work of several centuries, from the Renaissance to the present day. Therefore, they do not conform to a single style, but show the characteristics of the period in which each one was built.

The early residence of the Popes was, as we know, the Lateran Palace flanking the Basilica of the Saviour where the Holy Stairs were kept. Of this Palace there are several precious relics: a fresco attributed to Giotto, at present in the first right-hand nave as one enters the Basilica of St. John, which represents Boniface VIII proclaiming to the people the Jubilee of 1300; and the so-called Leonine Wall of the garden of the Holy Stairs, with a mosaic of the ninth century, restored in modern times, which shows the union of the two supreme powers, the Church and the Emperor, ruling the world under the protection of the Saviour. Although the Lateran was their regular residence, for the great liturgic solemnities and for the most important ceremonies, such as the Coronations of the Emperors, the Popes had, near the Basilica of St. Peter, smaller palaces and apartments. After the return from Avignon in the fifteenth century the Lateran was abandoned completely, and it became necessary to construct new buildings which would fit the requirements of daily living and correspond to the prestige of the Church.

The man who gave the major impulse to these constructions was Nicholas V (1447-1455). We owe to him the wings of the Palace which look, toward the West, on the Belvedere Court (page 63) and, toward the East, on the Court of San Damaso. Incorporated into the ancient buildings of Innocent III (1193-1216) and Nicholas III (1277-1280), these wings form a quadrangular structure which surrounds the Pappagallo Court and contains the apartments of Sixtus IV, Alexander Borgia, Julius II and Leo X. When the Sistine Chapel was added to this central nucleus by Sixtus IV (1471-1484) the concentration of great works of art in one place was complete. All the great masters, from Angelico to Pinturicchio, from Raphael to Michelangelo, created here their masterpieces; and the Italian Renaissance is present here in its greatest glory.

At about the same time, Innocent VIII (1484-1492) commissioned Giacomo Pietrasanta to construct a smaller building, designed by A. Pollaiolo, on the far side of the Vatican Hill which looks toward Mt. Marius: the Little Belvedere Palace (page 75). Julius II (1503-1513) had Bramante join this with the first building and with the Loggia overlooking the Court of San Damaso by means of a corridor, several floors high and about 1,000 feet long, with a terrace on top. Later on, Pius IV (1559-1565) had another similar corridor constructed toward the gardens, thus enclosing a rectangular area which formed the large Belvedere Court, closed on the South by the front of Nicholas V's palace and on the North by the Little Palace of Innocent VIII. To give to this northern side a good architectural line, Pius IV added a new building, designed by Pirro Ligorio, to the Little Palace of Innocent VIII; and there, in the center, a large niche was made, into which was transported, under Paul V (1605-1621), the famous Pigna di Bronzo, a pine cone of bronze which had been admired all through the Middle Ages in the Atrium of St. Peter's and had been also mentioned by Dante; hence the name of Nicchione della Pigna (page 71).

The area enclosed by these constructions was not even: for about 500 feet its level was about the same as that of the surrounding terrain, but then it mounted gradually by means of a series of stairs, until it reached the upper floor of the corridor. Therefore, the place was suitable for public shows, as was the custom in many Courts of the Renaissance, the audience being spread out on the stairs, at the windows and along the porticoes at the two sides. This was the Belvedere Theater, which is often mentioned in the chronicles and prints of the time. Twenty years later, the difference in level between the two parts gave the idea to Sixtus V (1585-1590) of erecting, at the points where the stairs began, a new transversal building in order to house there the Library of Sixtus IV, then confined to the floor beneath the Borgia Apartment. Thus the new Vatican Library came into being under the direction of the architect Domenico

64

Fontana. As it gradually grew larger, the Library, together with the Secret Archives, came to occupy the side galleries as far as the early Papal Palace on the South and the Palace of Pius IV on the North. The example given by Sixtus V was followed later by Pius VII (1800-1822) who, at the point where the stairs ended, had the architect Stern design the new wing (Braccio Nuovo) of the Museums of Sculpture (1817-1822). In this way the original Belvedere Court became divided into three parts: the lowest one kept for itself alone the name Belvedere, the third one took its name from the Pigna, while the middle one, between the Library and the Braccio Nuovo, was called the Library Court.

The principal reason for the erection of these buildings was to create adequate and suitable quarters to house books, documents and artistic and archaeologic objects. For the same reason Clement XIV (1769-1774) and Pius VI (1775-1799) undertook the construction of that group of galleries, adjoining the Little Palace of Innocent VIII and the Pigna Palace, which became the Museum of Sculpture, called after its founders the Museo Pio-Clementino. With the new monumental entrance to the Museums from the Viale Vaticano and with the construction of the Pinacoteca ordered by Pius XI (1922-1939) the Vatican Palace reached the northern edges of the hill, thus presenting to the traveler coming from Mt. Marius a varied and interesting outline of buildings which seems to invite him toward the incomparable treasures they contain.

But if the Palace grew so much in its ramifications toward the North, it acquired other and more important additions on the South and East, toward St. Peter's and the city. Alexander VI began by erecting the Borgia Tower, to which Pius V (1566-1572) added that structure which closes the Belvedere on the South and faces, on the opposite side, the Sistine Chapel and the Gardens. Between Alexander VI and Pius V, Julius II built the Loggias and the Bramante Corridor; and Paul III (1534-1550) constructed the Royal Hall and the Pauline Chapel which joined the Palace with St. Peter's Basilica, thus creating new problems for an easy access, resolved later by Bernini with the Royal Staircase. The next Pope, Julius III (1550-1555), began the superstructures on the Bramante Corridor — today the Lapidary Gallery — continued by Paul IV (1555-1559) and Urban VIII (1623-1644), where the Noble Guards now have their quarters. In these rooms, which look out over the Belvedere Court, theatrical performances were given under Julius III, last heir of the literary tastes and pageantry of Leo X: among the plays were Terence's *Eunuch* and Plautus's *Aulularia*, as well as others by contemporary authors.

However, the Popes who surpassed all the others were Gregory XIII (1572-1585) and Sixtus V (1585-1590). Gregory XIII conceived the idea of a building which, set at a right angle to the Bramante Loggias toward the East, would imitate their design and proportions. At the end of the building an open hall, dedicated to Bologna, looked toward Mt. Marius and the city: it was inaugurated in the Jubilee year, 1575, and from it, as from the Loggia of Raphael, there was a splendid panoramic view of Rome and the countryside, from Mt. Soratte, Mt. Gennaro and the Albani Hills to the Pontine Marshes and the sea. And in order to honor his native city and the study of astronomy and law, which he loved, he had Cherubino and Giovanni Alberti paint on the vault the sky with the stars and the Signs of the Zodiac, and, on the inside walls, the plan of Bologna and its environs, flanked by two historical scenes: on the left as you look, Gregory IX consigning the Decretals; on the right, Boniface VIII sanctioning the statutes of the University of Bologna. We see here an imitation of Raphael's frescoes, in the Stanza della Segnatura, which represent Justinian consigning the Pandects, and Gregory IX the Decretals. This was a building more than 130 feet tall, and its construction had required skill and boldness. But even more skill and boldness was shown by Gregory's successor, Sixtus V, and by his architect, Domenico Fontana.

To him we owe, not only the transportation and erection of the obelisk and the completion of Michelangelo's dome, but also the construction of that large palace, flanking the Braccio di Gregorio, which formed the third side of the Court of San Damaso and, pushing further to the East, constituted a solid block overlooking the hill and the city. Together with the recently-built apartments of Gregory XIII, this palace became the regular residence of the Popes and their court, and in it were installed the Secretariate of State and all the important administrative departments of the Holy See. The interior of the palace was arranged by the successors of Sixtus V, Popes Clement VIII Aldobrandini (1592-1605), Paul V Borghese (1605-1621) and Urban VIII Barberini (1623-1644); their coats of arms are visible over several doors, particularly on the second floor of the Loggias, the favorite dwelling of all Popes up to our times.

Little by little the most ancient parts ceased to be used as private residences. The major Chapels, the Sistine and the Pauline, kept their religious character, while the minor ones and the apartments where the Renaissance Popes had lived were opened to scholars and art lovers who, even before the establishment of the Museums and Galleries, used to come to Rome from all parts of Europe and were free to visit them.

Belvedere Court from the side the Library of Sixtus V - Patio del Belvedere (lado de la Biblioteca de Sixto V)
Cour du Belvédère du côté de la Bibliothèque de Sixte V - Cortile del Belvedere dal lato della Biblioteca di Sisto V

El Palacio Vaticano es un conjunto de construcciones que, por resumir el trabajo de muchos siglos, desde el Renacimiento a los períodos sucesivos, no corresponden a un dibujo único y guardan pués las huellas características de los distintos períodos. La morada primitiva de los Papas fué en el Palacio de Letrán, flanqueado por la Basílica del Salvador, que custodiaba también a la Escalera Santa. Reliquias preciosas de este Palacio son: un fresco atribuido a Giotto, representante Bonifacio VIII que proclama al pueblo el Jubiléo de 1300; este fresco se ve ahora aplicado al primer pilar de la primera nave a la derecha de quién entre en la Basílica de San Juán; además, una gran pared absidada en el jardín de la Escalera Santa, que mira hacia la puerta y las murallas, dicha pared del Triclinio Leoniano, sobre la cual un precioso mosaico del IX siglo, modernamente restaurado, ilustra, en sus quadros laterales, la unión de los poderes supremos de la Iglesia y del Imperio que, bajo la protección del Salvador, gobiernan al mundo. Pero, si el Letrán era la morada ordinaria, para las grandes fiestas litúrgicas y para las ceremonias más importantes, como la encoronación de los soberanos, los Pontífices tenían, cerca de la Basílica Vaticana, palacios menores y aposentos de habitación; y cuando, después de la vuelta de los Papas de Aviñón en el siglo XV, el

Palacio de Letrán fué abandonado, volviéronse necesarias nuevas construcciones que, sin rivalizar con el antiguo Patriarquio o tanto menos con la majestuosa ciudadela de Aviñón, fueran suficientes para los requerimientos de la vida de cada dia y el prestigio del gobierno de la Iglesia. Quien más fomentó a estas nuevas construcciones fué Nicolas V (1447-1455), y a él debemos aquellas alas del palacio que miran a tramontana, hacia el patio del Belvedere (pág. 63) y, a levante, hacia el patio de San Dámaso; estas alas, incorporadas con los antiguos edificios de Inocencio III (1193-1216) y Nicolas III (1277-1280), forman una especie de cuadrilátero que encierra el así llamado patio del Papagayo, donde también estuvieron los aposentos de Sixto IV, de Alejandro Borja, de Julio II y de León X. A este nucleo central Sixto IV (1471-1484) le añadió la Capilla Sixtina y así fueron aunados en el mismo punto los sagrarios del arte donde sobresalen los nombres de los grandes maestros que del Angélico al Pinturicchio, de Rafael a Miguel Ángel, crearon aquí sus obras, y la pintura italiana del Renacimiento celebra sus triunfos máximos.

Casi contemporaneamente, sobre una extremidad de la Colina Vaticana hacia Monte Mario, Inocencio VIII (1484-1492) encargaba a Giacomo Pietrasanta, sobre dibujo de A. Pollaiolo, la construcción de un edificio menor, llamado el Palacete de Belvedere (pág. 75), que Julio II (1503-1513) mandó enlazar con el primerio y con la logia de frente al patio de San Dámaso, mediante un corredor, obra de Bramante, que tenía distintos pisos, largo cerca de 300 metros y cubierto por un balcon. Más tarde Pio IV (1559-1565), a imitación de este corredor, mandó edificar paralelamente otro hacia los jardines, delimitando así un área rectangular que formó el gran patio de Belvedere, cerrado a mediodía por el frente del palacio de Nicolas V y a tramontana por el Palacete de Inocencio VIII. Para dar a este frente una línea arquitectónica digna del ambiente, al Palacete de Inocencio VIII Pio IV, bajo un dibujo de Pirro Ligorio, le mandó añadir un nuevo edificio, en el centro del cual fué sacado un gran nicho, donde, bajo Pablo V (1605-1621), fué transportada la afamada Piña de Bronce, que había quedado por toda la edad media en el atrio de San Pedro, como la menciona también Dante; de allí el nombre de « Nicchione della Pigna », o « Nicho de la Piña » (pág. 71). El área que resultaba de estas construcciones no estaba toda sobre el mismo plano. En su primera parte, por un largo de cerca de 150 metros, estaba más o menos al nivel del terreno circunyacente, luego subía gradualmente con una serie de graderías hasta alcanzar al piso superior del corredor. Habíase así el ambiente apto, según las constumbres de las cortes del Renacimiento, para representaciones públicas, a que los convidados asistían desde las graderías hacia tramontana, desde los balcones del palacio hacia mediodía, y desde las ventanas y los pórticos alineados a lo largo de los lados. Es esto el teatro de Belvedere, que está muchas veces mencionado en las cronicas y en las estampas de la época.

El desnivel entre la parte inferior y la superior del Nicho de la Piña, veinte años más tarde, le sugerió a Sixto V (1585-1590) la idea de construir, en el punto donde empezaban las graderías, un nuevo edificio transversal, para colocar allí a la Biblioteca de Sixto IV, que estaba entonces alojada en el piso inferior debajo del aposento Borja. Así, bajo la dirección del arquitecto Domenico Fontana, edificóse la nueva Biblioteca Vaticana, que sucesivamente fué ensanchada hasta ocupar, junto con el Archivo secreto, las galerías laterales y alcanzar, hacia mediodía, el palacio pontificio originario, y, hacia tramontana, el palacio de Pio IV y el Nicho de la Piña. El ejemplo de Sixto V fué seguido más tarde por Pio VII (1800-1822) que, en el punto donde terminaban las graderías y empezaba el piso más elevado del patio, encargó al arquitecto Stern la construcción del Brazo Nuevo de los Museos de Escultura (1817-1822). El patio original de Belvedere quedó así divido en tres partes: la primera, abajo, guardó para sí sola el nombre de Belvedere; la tercera, arriba, tuvo el de patio de la Piña; mientras que a la segunda, colocada entre la Biblioteca y el Brazo Nuevo, le tocó el nombre de Patio de la Biblioteca.

La razón principal que determinó a la erección de estos edificios fué la de crear ambientes aptos y suficientes para acoger libros, documentos y monumentos artísticos al servicio de los estudiosos; y la misma razón fué la que empujó a Clemente XIV (1769-1774) y a Pio VI (1775-1799) a idear la construcción de aquel conjunto de galerías que, arrimado al Palacete de Inocencio VIII y al patio de la Piña, alojó el Museo de Escultura, también conocido como Museo Pio-Clementino. Con el nuevo monumental ingreso a los Museos desde la Alameda Vaticana, y con el edificio de la Pinacoteca, encargado por Pio XI (1922-1939), el Palacio Vaticano alcanzó a los bordes extremos de la colina hacia tramontana, presentando al viajero que se asome desde Monte Mario — de las murallas almenadas del Palacete de Inocencio VIII a las Cúpulas de la Sala Redonda, de la Cruz Griega y de la Biga — una línea movida de edificios que hace adivinar y desear una colección de tesoros todavía sumidos en el encanto del misterio.

Aún más importantes fueron los ensanches del palacio a mediodía y a oriente, hacia San Pedro y hacia la ciudad. Empezó Alejandro VI con la torre Borja, a la que Pio V (1566-1572) le añadió aquel cuerpo de edificio que cierra a mediodía el Belvedere y esta enfrente de la Capilla Sixtina y de los Jardines. Entre Alejandro VI y Pio V injértase la actividad de Julio II con las Logias y con el Corredor de Bramante, luego la de Pablo III (1534-1550) con la sala Regia y la Capilla Paulina que, empalmando el Palacio con la Basílica, crearon nuevos problemas de construcción, resueltos más tarde por Bernini con la Escalera Regia. Sucede Julio III (1550-1555) que inaugura a los sobrealzados del Corredor de Bramante — hoy Galería Lapidaria — continuados por Pablo IV (1555-1559) y por Urbano VIII (1623-1644), donde ahora hay el cuartel de los Guardas Nobles. Aquí, en los primeros salones que miran hacia el Patio de Belvedere, bajo Julio III, el último heredero de los gustos literario y del fausto de León X, representáronse, junto con dramas de autores contemporáneos, el *Eunuco* de Terencio y la *Aulularia* de Plauto. Pero quienes les sobrepasaron a todos fueron Gregorio XIII (1572-1585) y Sixto V (1585-1590). Gregorio XIII concebió la idea de un edificio que, injertándose en ángulo recto con las Logias de Bramante hacia levante reprodujera las proporciones y la línea de las Logias mismas; y en la cabezera del edificio que mira hacia los Borgos, dedico él a Boloña un salón abierto con arcos hacia Monte Mario y la ciudad; fué esto inaugurado en el año de jubiléo de 1575, y desde ello, como desde la Logia de Rafael, gozábase la vista panorámica de Roma y de todo el agro romano, desde los Montes Soratte, Gennaro y las Colinas Albanas hasta los Pantanos Pontinos y el mar. Y para que en este salón quedara memoria de su ciudad natal, así como de las ciencias astrónomicas y jurídicas que prefería, mandó el Papa que los hermanos Cherubino y Juan Alberti pintasen en la bóveda el cielo estrellado con los signos zodiacales y, en las paredes sin arcos, la plantilla de la campaña de Boloña y la de la ciudad, flanqueada por dos escenas históricas: a la derecha Bonifacio VIII que sanciona a los estatutos de la Universidad de Boloña, donde es clara la imitación de los frescos de Rafael en la Cámara de la Signatura, que representan la entrega de las Pandectas de Justiniano y de las Decretales por el mismo Gregorio IX que, a la izquierda, está aquí representado en el acto de entregar el código de las Decretales. En esta construcción el problema era de erigir a un edificio que medía cerca de 40 metros de altura a la base, requeriendo pués calidades no comunes de atrevimiento y de técnica en los arquitectos; las pruebas, ya excelentes, de los arquitectos de Gregorio XIII fueron aún sobrepasadas por el arquitecto preferido de su sucesor Sixto V, Doménico Fontana. A los trofeos conqueridos con el transporte y la erección del obelisco y con el haber dado remate a la cúpula de Miguel Ángel, añadio él el laurel arquitectónico representado por la construcción del gigantesco palacio que, arrimándose al Brazo de Gregorio, marcó el tercero lado del Patio de San Damaso y, adelantándose más hacia levante, formó el masizo cuadrilátero que domina a la colina Vaticana y a la ciudad. No quedaba pués sino cuidar el arreglo interior del nuevo palacio que, junto con los aposentos recién construidos por Gregorio XIII, volvióse la morada actual de los Pontífices y de su séquito, de la Secretaria de Estado y de las Oficinas administrativas de la Santa Sede y en general el centro de gobierno de la Iglesia universal. Esta fué la tarea de los sucesores de Sixto V, Clemente VIII Aldobrandini (1592-1605), Pablo V Borghese (1605-1621) y Urbano VIII Barberini (1623-1644), cuyas empresas heráldicas aparecen a menudo sobre los dinteles de las puertas y en las decoraciones del palacio, especialmente en las salas del segundo piso de las Logias, el piso preferido por los Papas como morada hasta nuestros dias.

Las partes más antiguas acabaron gradualmente de ser empleadas como moradas particulares. Guardaron a su carácter religioso las Capillas Sixtina y Paulina, mientras que las capillas menores, así como los aposentos a ellas conectados, que habian sido las moradas de los Papas en el Renacimiento, fueron abiertos a los extranjeros y a los estudiosos de arte y de historia que, aún antes de la institución de los Museos y de las Galerías, eso es, antes de la segunda mitad del siglo XVIII, aunábanse en Roma desde toda Europa, y podían así visitarlos libremente.

Pigna Court - Patio de la Piña
Cour de la Pigna - Cortile della Pigna

Le Palais du Vatican est un ensemble d'édifices qui sous leur aspect actuel résument le travail de plusieurs siècles, à partir de la Renaissance, et par conséquent ne répondent pas à un plan unique mais conservent en chacun de leurs éléments les empreintes caractéristiques du temps passé.

La résidence primitive des Papes était jadis, comme on sait, au Palais de Latran accolé à la Basilique du Sauveur qui conservait également la *Scala Santa*. Parmi les restes précieux de ce Palais on voit une fresque attribuée à Giotto, représentant Boniface VIII qui proclame au peuple le Jubilé de 1300; cette fresque se trouve maintenant appliquée au premier pilier de la première nef à droite quand on pénètre dans la Basilique de Saint-Jean; en outre un grand mur de chevet du jardin de la Scala Santa, qui regarde vers la porte et les murailles, mur appelé du Triclinio Leoniano, sur lequel une mosaïque précieuse du IX<sup>e</sup> siècle, récemment restaurée, montre dans ses tableaux latéraux l'union des pouvoirs suprêmes de l'Eglise et de l'Empire, qui, sous la protection du Sauveur, gouvernent le monde. Pour les grandes fêtes liturgiques et pour les principales cérémonies, comme pour le couronnement des souverains, les Pontifes avaient auprès de la Basilique Vaticane des palais plus petits et des appartements d'habitation. Au XV<sup>e</sup> siècle, après le retour d'Avignon, quand le palais de Latran fut aban-

71

donné, l'on dut recourir à de nouvelles constructions capables, je ne dis pas de rivaliser avec l'ancien Patriarcat et moins encore avec l'imposant Château d'Avignon, mais de répondre aux exigences de la vie quotidienne et au prestige du gouvernement de l'Eglise. Le pape qui donna le plus d'impulsion à cette entreprise fut Nicolas V (1447-1455). On lui doit les bâtiments qui donnent au couchant sur la cour du Belvédère (page 63) et au levant sur la cour de Saint-Damase et qui, incorporés aux anciens édifices d'Innocent III (1193-1216) et de Nicolas III (1277-1280), forment une espèce de quadrilatère qui renferme la cour dite du Perroquet, où furent aussi les appartements de Sixte IV, d'Alexandre Borgia, Jules II et Léon X. A ce noyau central Sixte IV (1471-1484) ajouta la Chapelle Sixtine et c'est ainsi que vinrent se réunir sur le même point ces sanctuaires d'art ou brillent les noms des grands maîtres qui de l'Angelico au Pinturicchio, de Raphaël à Michel-Ange ont ici créé leurs chefs-d'œuvre et dans lesquels la peinture italienne de la Renaissance fête ses principaux triomphes.

A peu près à la même époque, sur une extrémité de la colline vaticane vers Monte Mario, Innocent VIII (1484-1492) faisait construire par Giacomo Pietrasanta, sur plan dessiné par A. Pollaiolo, un édifice de moindres dimensions: le Petit Belvédère (page 75) que Jules II (1503-1513) fit relier par Bramante au premier et à la loge qui regarde la cour de Saint-Damase au moyen d'un corridor de plusieurs étages et long d'environ trois cents mètres, couvert d'une terrasse. Plus tard Pie IV (1552-1565), à l'image de ce corridor en fit construire parallèlement un autre vers les jardins, délimitant ainsi un espace rectangulaire qui forma la grande cour du Belvédère, fermée au midi par la façade du Palais de Nicolas V et au couchant par le Petit Belvédère d'Innocent VIII. Pour donner ensuite à cette façade septentrionale une ligne architecturale digne du milieu, Pie II ajouta au Petit Belvédère d'Innocent VIII un nouveau bâtiment conçu d'après les plans de Pirro Ligorio, et l'on creusa au centre une grande niche où fut transportée au temps de Paul V (1605-1621) la fameuse Pomme de pin en bronze admirée par tout le Moyen âge sous le porche de Saint-Pierre et mentionnée même par Dante. La niche dès lors fut appelée « della Pigna » (page 71).

L'aire aménagée par ces constructions n'était pas toute sur le même plan. Tout d'abord, sur une longueur d'environ 150 m., elle se trouvait à peu près au niveau du sol avoisinant, puis elle s'élevait lentement par une série de gradins jusqu'à l'étage le plus haut du corridor. On avait ainsi un cadre adapté, selon l'usage des cours de la Renaissance, pour les spectacles publics auxquels les invités assistaient sur des gradins au nord, des balcons du palais au midi, et des fenêtres et des portiques alignés sur les côtés. C'est le théâtre du Belvédère qui se trouve mentionné plus d'une fois dans la chronique et sur les estampes du temps.

La dénivellation entre la partie inférieure et la partie supérieure de la Niche della Pigna suggéra vingt ans plus tard à Sixte-Quint (1585-1590) l'idée d'ériger à l'endroit où commençaient les degrés un nouvel édifice transversal, où aménager la bibliothèque reléguée alors à l'étage au dessous de l'appartement des Borgia. C'est ainsi que sous la direction de l'architecte Fontana surgit la Bibliothèque Vaticane qui devait s'agrandir par la suite et petit à petit occuper, avec les Archives secrètes, les galeries latérales jusqu'à rejoindre vers le midi l'ancien palais pontifical, et vers le nord le palais de Pie

IV et la grande Niche della Pigna. L'exemple de Sixte-Quint plus tard fut suivi par Pie VII (1800-1822) qui, à l'endroit où cessaient les gradins et où commençait le plan le plus élevé de la cour, fit ériger par l'architecte Stern la nouvelle aile des Musées de Sculpture (1817-1822). De cette manière l'ancienne cour du Belvédère resta divisée en trois parties : la première en bas garda pour elle seule le nom de Belvédère, la troisième en haut reçut celui della Pigna et la deuxième, située entre la Bibliothèque et le Braccio Nuovo, reçut celui de Cour de la Bibliothèque.

La raison principale qui détermina l'érection de ces édifices était de créer des pièces adaptées et suffisantes pour mettre à la disposition des lecteurs livres, documents et monuments d'art et d'archéologie ; et cette même raison encouragea Clément XIV (1769-1774) et Pie VI (1775-1799) à la construction de cet ensemble de galeries qui, adossé au petit palais d'Innocent VIII et à celui de la Pigna, est devenu le siège du Musée de Sculpture, appelé par ses fondateurs Musée Pio-Clementino. Avec la nouvelle entrée monumentale des Musées du Vatican par l'Avenue Vaticane et avec les bâtiments de la Pinacothèque ordonnés par Pie XI (1922-1939), le Palais Vatican atteignit les bords les plus éloignés de la colline vers le nord, présentant au voyageur qui arrive de Monte Mario, depuis les murs crénelés du petit palais d'Innocent VIII jusqu'aux coupoles de la Salle Ronde, de la Croix-Grecque et de la Bige, une ligne mouvementée d'édifices qui fait entrevoir et désirer une collection de trésors encore enveloppés dans le charme du mystère.

Mais si le Palais avait reçu de tels accroissements dans ses ramifications vers le nord, il en est d'autres et plus importants au midi et à l'est vers Saint-Pierre et vers la ville. Alexandre VI commença par la tour des Borgia, à laquelle Pie V (1566-1572) ajouta ce corps de bâtiment qui clôt au midi le Belvédère et fait face, du côté opposé, à la Chapelle Sixtine et aux Jardins. Entre Alexandre VI et Pie V va s'insérer l'activité de Jules II avec les loges et avec le corridor de Bramante ; puis celle de Paul III (1534-1550) avec la Salle Royale et la Chapelle Pauline qui relient le palais à la Basilique et créent pour les accès de nouveaux problèmes éditaires qui seront résolus plus tard par Bernini avec l'Escalier Royal. Succède Jules II (1550-1555) qui inaugure les surélévations du corridor de Bramante — aujourd'hui Galerie Lapidaire — continuées par Paul IV (1555-1559) et par Urbain VIII (1623-1644), où se trouve maintenant le Quartier des Gardes-Nobles. C'est ici, dans les premières salles du Quartier qui donnent sur la cour du Belvédère, que sous Jules III, dernier héritier des goûts littéraires et du faste de Léon X, furent représentés, en même temps que les drames d'auteurs contemporains, l'*Eunuque* de Térence et l'*Aululaire* de Plaute. Mais les pontifes qui se surpassèrent ont été Grégoire XIII (1572-1585) et Sixte-Quint (1585-1590). Grégoire XIII conçut l'idée d'un bâtiment accouplé en angle droit aux loges de Bramante dans la direction du levant, dont il devait reproduire les proportions et les plans ; et en tête de l'édifice qui regarde les « Borghi » il consacra à Bologne une salle à arcades ouvertes dans la direction de Monte Mario et de la ville. De cette salle inaugurée l'année du Jubilé de 1575, on avait, comme de la loge de Raphaël, une vue panoramique de la ville et de toute la campagne romaine depuis les cimes du Soracte, de Monte Gennaro et des collines d'Albe jusqu'aux marais pontins et à la mer. Et

73

pour que dans cette salle restât le souvenir de sa ville natale et des sciences astronomiques et juridiques, objet particulier de sa prédilection, il fit peindre par les frères Cherubino et Giovanni Alberti, sous la voûte, le ciel étoilé ave les signes du Zodiaque et, sur les murs non ouverts par des arceaux, le plan du comté de Bologne et celui de la ville accompagné de deux scènes historiques: à gauche du spectateur, Grégoire remettant le code des Décrétales; à droite, Boniface VIII sanctionnant les statuts de cette Université des études, où apparait manifeste l'imitation des fresques de Raphaël dans la Salle de la Signature, qui représentent la remise des Pandectes de Justinien et des Décrétales par le même Pontife Grégoire IX. Quant à cette dernière construction il s'agit d'un édifice qui mesurait à partir de la base environ 40 m. d'altitude, et exigeait de la part des constructeurs des qualités peu communes de hardiesse et de technique. Mais les performances excellentes fournies par les architectes de Grégoire XIII furent de bien loin surpassées par le successeur Sixte-Quint et par son architecte favori Dominique Fontana.

Aux trophées conquis avec le transport et l'érection de l'obélisque et avec l'achèvement de la coupole de Michel-Ange, il ajouta celui du gigantesque palais qui, accolé à l'aile de Grégoire, constitue le troisième côté de la cour de Saint-Damase et, s'étendant par delà au levant, forme un quadrilatère massif qui domine la colline vaticane et la ville. Après quoi il n'y avait plus qu'à pourvoir à l'aménagement intérieur du nouveau palais devenu avec la récente construction des appartements de Grégoire XIII la résidence actuelle des Souverains Pontifes et de leur cour, de la Secrétairerie d'Etat, des bureaux d'administration du Saint Siège et en général le centre du gouvernement de l'Eglise universelle. Ce fut la tâche des successeurs de Sixte-Quint, de Clément VIII Aldobrandini (1592-1605), de Paul V Borghese (1605-1621) et d'Urbain VIII Barberini (1623-1644), dont les devises héraldiques reviennent maintes fois sur les architraves des portes et dans les peintures décoratives du palais, notamment dans les salles du deuxième étage des loges, celui que tous les Papes ont préféré pour leur demeure jusqu'à nos jours.

Les parties les plus anciennes ont cessé peu à peu d'être des habitations privées. Les chapelles principales, comme la Sixtine et la Pauline, ont gardé leur caractère religieux, tandis que les secondaires et les appartements juxtaposés, qui avaient été la résidence quotidienne des Papes de la Renaissance, furent ouverts au public et aux spécialistes d'art et d'histoire qui, même avant l'institution des Musées et des Galeries, c'est-à-dire dès la seconde moitié du XVIIIᵉ siècle, accouraient à Rome de tous les coins de l'Europe et pouvaient les visiter librement.

Little Palace of Innocent VIII - Palacete de Inocencio VIII
Petit Palais d'Innocent VIII - Palazzetto d'Innocenzo VIII

Il Palazzo Vaticano è un complesso di edifici che, nel loro assetto attuale, riassumono il lavoro di parecchi secoli, dal Rinascimento in poi, e non corrispondono perciò ad un unico disegno e conservano, parte a parte, le impronte caratteristiche del tempo trascorso.

Come si sa, la residenza primitiva dei Papi fu nel Palazzo del Laterano, affiancato alla Basilica del Salvatore che custodiva pure la Scala Santa. Reliquie preziose di questo Palazzo sono: un affresco attribuito a Giotto, rappresentante Bonifacio VIII che proclama al popolo il Giubileo del '300 e che si vede ora applicato al primo pilastro della prima navata di destra di chi entra nella Basilica di S. Giovanni; inoltre una grande parete absidata del giardino della Scala Santa, che guarda verso la porta e le mura, detta del Triclinio Leoniano, sulla quale un prezioso mosaico del IX secolo, moder- namente restaurato, nei suoi quadri laterali mostra la unione dei supremi poteri della Chiesa e dell'Impero, che, sotto la protezione del Salvatore, governano il mondo. Ma se al Laterano era la residenza ordinaria, per le grandi feste liturgiche e per le ceri- monie maggiori, come per l'incoronazione dei sovrani, i Pontefici avevano presso la Basilica Vaticana palazzi minori ed appartamenti d'abitazione; e quando, dopo il ritorno da Avignone, nel secolo XV, il palazzo del Laterano venne abbandonato, si resero necessarie nuove costruzioni che emulassero, non dico l'antico Patriarchio e tanto meno l'imponente rocca di Avignone, ma rispondessero alle esigenze della vita quotidiana e al prestigio del governo della Chiesa. Chi diede il maggiore impulso a queste fabbriche fu Niccolò V (1447-1455), e a lui si devono quelle ali del palazzo che guardano a tramontana sul cortile del Belvedere (pag. 63) e a levante sul cortile di S. Damaso e che, incorporate con gli edifici antichi d'Innocenzo III (1193-1216) e Niccolò III (1277-1280), formano una specie di quadrilatero che racchiude il cosidetto cortile del Pappagallo e dove furono anche gli appartamenti di Sisto IV, di Alessandro Borgia, Giulio II e Leone X. A questo nucleo centrale Sisto IV (1471-1484) aggiunse la Cappella Sistina e così vennero a riunirsi nel medesimo punto i sacrari dell'arte, in cui brillano i nomi dei grandi maestri che, dall'Angelico al Pinturicchio, da Raffaello a Michelangelo, hanno creato qui i loro capolavori, e la pittura italiana del Rinascimento celebra i suoi massimi trionfi.

Quasi contemporaneamente, sopra una estremità del Colle Vaticano verso Monte Mario, Innocenzo VIII (1484-1492) faceva costruire da Giacomo Pietrasanta, su disegno di A. Pollaiolo, un edificio minore, detto il Palazzetto di Belvedere (pag. 75), che Giulio II (1503-1513) fece congiungere dal Bramante col primo e con la loggia prospiciente il cortile di S. Damaso, mediante un corridore di diversi piani e lungo circa trecento metri, coperto da una terrazza. Più tardi Pio IV (1559-1565), a somiglianza di questo corridore ne fece costruire parallelamente un altro verso i giardini, delimitando così un'area rettangolare che formò il grande cortile di Belvedere, chiuso a mezzodì dalla fronte del palazzo di Niccolò V e a tramontana dal Palazzetto di Innocenzo VIII. Per dare poi a questa fronte settentrionale una linea architettonica degna dell'ambiente, al palazzetto di Innocenzo VIII fu da Pio IV aggiunto, con disegno di Pirro Ligorio, un nuovo fabbricato, ed ivi al centro venne ricavata una grande nicchia, nella quale fu trasportata, ai tempi di Paolo V (1605-1621), la famosa Pigna di Bronzo, ammirata per tutto il medio-evo nell'atrio di S. Pietro e ricordata pure da Dante; donde il nome di Nicchione della Pigna (pag. 71).

L'area risultante da queste costruzioni non era tutta sullo stesso piano. In un primo tratto, per la lunghezza di circa 150 m. era al livello press'a poco del terreno circostante, poi saliva lentamente con una serie di gradinate fino a raggiungere il piano superiore del Corridore. Si aveva così un ambiente adatto, secondo l'uso delle Corti del Rinascimento, per pubblici spettacoli, a cui gli invitati assistevano dalle gradinate, verso tramontana, dai balconi del palazzo a mezzodì e dalle finestre e dai portici allineati sui fianchi. E' il teatro di Belvedere, che si trova più volte menzionato nelle cronache e nelle stampe del tempo.

Il dislivello tra la parte inferiore e quella superiore del Nicchione della Pigna suggerì vent'anni dopo a Sisto V (1585-1590) l'idea di erigere nel punto in cui cominciavano le gradinate, un nuovo edificio trasversale, dove sistemare la Biblioteca di Sisto IV, confinata allora nel piano sottostante all'Appartamento Borgia. Così sotto la direzione dell'architetto Domenico Fontana sorse la nuova Biblioteca Vaticana che successivamente s'ingrandì e poco per volta occupò insieme con l'Archivio segreto le gallerie laterali fino a raggiungere verso il mezzodì il primitivo palazzo pontificio, e verso tramontana il palazzo di Pio IV del Nicchione della Pigna. L'esempio di Sisto V fu seguito più tardi da Pio VII (1800-1822), il quale, nel punto in cui finivano le gradinate e cominciava il piano più elevato del cortile, fece erigere dall'architetto Stern il Braccio Nuovo dei Musei di Scultura (1817-1822). In tal modo l'originario cortile di Belvedere restò diviso in tre parti: la prima in basso mantenne per sè sola il nome di Belvedere, la terza in alto ebbe quella della Pigna, e la seconda, posta in mezzo tra la Biblioteca e il Braccio Nuovo, ebbe quello di cortile della Biblioteca.

La ragione principale che determinò l'erezione di questi edifici fu quella di creare ambienti adatti e sufficienti per accogliere libri, documenti e monumenti artistici ed archeologici in servizio degli studiosi; e la ragione medesima fu quella che incoraggiò Clemente XIV (1769-1774) e Pio VI (1775-1799) alla costruzione di quel complesso di gallerie che, addossato al Palazzetto d'Innocenzo VIII e a quello della Pigna, divenne sede del Museo di Scultura, detto dai suoi fondatori Museo Pio-Clementino. Col nuovo monumentale ingresso ai Musei dal Viale Vaticano e coll'edificio della Pinacoteca ordinati da Pio XI (1922-1939), il Palazzo Vaticano raggiunse gli orli estremi della collina verso tramontana, presentando al viaggiatore che si affaccia da Monte Mario — dalle mura merlate del Palazzetto d'Innocenzo VIII alle cupole della Sala Rotonda, della Croce Greca e della Biga — una linea movimentata di edifici che fa intravedere e desiderare un'accolta di tesori ancora avvolti nel fascino del mistero.

Ma se tanti incrementi aveva avuto il Palazzo nelle sue diramazioni verso tramontana, altri e più importanti ne ebbe a mezzodì e a oriente verso S. Pietro e verso la città. Cominciò Alessandro VI con la torre Borgia, a cui Pio V (1566-1572) aggiunse quel corpo di fabbricato che chiude a mezzodì il Belvedere e fronteggia dal lato opposto la Cappella Sistina e i Giardini. Tra Alessandro VI e Pio V s'inserisce l'attività di Giulio II con le Logge e con il Corridore di Bramante, poi quella di Paolo III (1534-1550) con la Sala Regia e la Cappella Paolina che congiungono il palazzo con la Basilica e creano per gli accessi nuovi problemi edilizi risolti più tardi dal Bernini con la Scala Regia. Succede Giulio III (1550-1555), che inaugura le sopraelevazioni del Corridore di Bramante — oggi Galleria Lapidaria — continuate da Paolo IV (1555-1559) e da Urbano VIII (1623-1644), dove ora è il quartiere delle Guardie Nobili. Qui nelle prime sale del quartiere che prospettano il Cortile di Belvedere, sotto Giulio III, ultimo erede dei gusti letterari e del fasto di Leone X, furono rappresentate, insieme con drammi di autori contemporanei, l'*Eunuco* di Terenzio e l'*Aulularia* di Plauto. Ma chi tutti li sorpassò furono Gregorio XIII (1572-1585) e Sisto V (1585-1590). Gregorio XIII concepì l'idea di un fabbricato che innestandosi ad angolo retto con le Logge di Bramante in direzione di levante, ne riproducesse le proporzioni e il disegno; e nella testata dell'edificio che guarda i Borghi, dedicò a Bologna una sala aperta con archi verso Monte Mario e verso la città. Inaugurata nell'anno del giubileo del 1575, e dalla quale come dalla Loggia di Raffaello, si aveva una vista panoramica dell'Urbe e di tutta la campagna romana, dalle cime del Soratte, di monte Gennaro e dei colli Albani fino alle paludi pontine e al mare. E perchè in questa sala restasse memoria della sua città natale, e delle scienze astronomiche e giuridiche da lui predilette, vi fece dipingere dai fratelli Cherubino e Giovanni Alberti, nella volta, il cielo stellato coi segni dello Zodiaco e, sulle pareti non aperte da archi, la pianta del contado di Bologna e quella della città fiancheggiata da due scene storiche: a sinistra di chi guarda Gregorio IX che consegna il codice delle Decretali; a destra Bonifacio VIII che sancisce gli statuti di quella Università degli studi, dove è manifesta l'imitazione degli affreschi di Raffaello nella Stanza della Segnatura, che rappresentano la consegna delle Pandette di Giustiniano e delle Decretali da parte del medesimo Gregorio IX. Si trattava in questa costruzione di un edificio che misurava dalla base circa 40 m. di altezza ed esigeva dai costruttori qualità non comuni di ardimento e di tecnica. Ma le prove eccellenti date dagli architetti di Gregorio XIII furono di gran lunga superate dal successore Sisto V e dal suo architetto preferito Domenico Fontana.

Ai trofei conquistati col trasporto e l'erezione dell'obelisco e col portare a compimento la cupola di Michelangelo egli aggiunse quello del gigantesco palazzo che, affiancandosi al Braccio di Gregorio, segnò il terzo lato del Cortile di S. Damaso e, spingendosi più oltre verso levante, formò un massiccio quadrilatero che sovrasta il colle Vaticano e la Città. Dopo di che non restava che curare la sistemazione interna del nuovo palazzo, il quale insieme con gli appartamenti di recente costruzione di Gregorio XIII, divenne residenza attuale dei Pontefici e della loro corte, della Segreteria di Stato e degli Uffici amministrativi della S. Sede, e in generale il centro di governo della Chiesa universale. Questo fu il compito dei successori di Sisto V, di Clemente VIII Aldobrandini (1592-1605), di Paolo V Borghese (1605-1621) e di Urbano VIII Barberini (1623-1644), le cui imprese araldiche ritornano più volte sugli architravi delle porte e nelle decorazioni pittoriche del palazzo, specialmente nelle sale del secondo piano delle Logge, quello preferito per loro dimora da tutti i Papi sino ai tempi nostri.

Le parti più antiche cessarono poco per volta di essere abitazioni private. Mantennero il loro carattere religioso le Cappelle maggiori Sistina e Paolina, laddove quelle minori e gli appartamenti connessi che erano stati residenza quotidiana dei Papi del Rinascimento, furono aperti agli stranieri e agli studiosi d'arte e di storia, che prima ancora dell'istituzione dei Musei e delle Gallerie, cioè fino alla seconda metà del secolo XVIII, accorrevano a Roma da ogni parte dell'Europa e potevano liberamente visitarli.

Court of San Damaso: Belvedere Loggias - Patio de San Damaso: Logias de Belvedere
Cour de S. Damase: Loges du Belvédère - Cortile di S. Damaso: Loggie di Belvedere

Bramante Staircase - Escalera de Bramante - Escalier de Bramante - Scala di Bramante

Royal Staircase - Escalera Regia - Escalier Royal - Scala Regia

Sistine Chapel: Exterior, side view - Capilla Sixtina: Exterior visto de lado
Chapelle Sixtine: Extérieur vu de côté - Cappella Sistina: Esterno visto di fianco

THE  CHAPEL  OF  NICOLAS  V

LA  CAPILLA  NICOLINA

LA  CHAPELLE  DE  NICOLAS  V

LA  CAPPELLA  NICOLINA

Beato Angelico: *Ordination of St. Lawrence* (detail) - Beato Angélico: *Ordenación de San Lorenzo* (detalle)
Fra Angelico: *Ordination de Saint Laurent* (détail) - Beato Angelico: *Ordinazione di S. Lorenzo* (particolare)

This Chapel, with its frescoes painted by Beato Angelico under Nicholas V between 1448 and 1450, is the oldest now in existence, since the one painted for Eugene IV in 1445-1447 was destroyed when the Royal Hall was built. In the beginning it was not a chapel but a study that the great humanist Pope wanted for his own use: it was made out of a tower of Nicholas III's palace wich was incorporated into the new building erected by him as a more suitable and spacious dwelling for the Popes. Religious paintings were not out of place even in a study, as in those times they were considered appropriate also in secular places. In this particular case no better subjects could be found, since St. Lawrence, as a deacon, was revered as protector of archives and libraries; and St. Stephen was associated with him in the ecclesiastic functions and worship. The lives of the two deacons are described in two parallel sections on three walls of the chapel; the fourth wall is taken up by the altar and a large window. On the four arches of the vault are painted the Evangelists with their symbols, and on the artificial niches underneath, the Doctors of the Church. In the upper area, framed by the arches, are the episodes in the life of St. Stephen. Starting at the left and continuing to the right we see: St. Peter conferring on him the deaconship and handing him the chalice; St. Stephen distributing alms to the poor; then, on the next wall, the Saint discussing with the Hebrews in a public place, while further to the right we see him before the judges of the Sanhedrin who are pronouncing the sentence

Beato Angelico: *St. Lawrence before the Emperor* (detail) - Beato Angélico: *San Lorenzo delante del Emperador* (detalle)
Fra Angelico: *Saint Laurent devant l'Empereur* (détail) - Beato Angelico: *S. Lorenzo davanti all'Imperatore* (particolare)

of death; on the third wall, St. Stephen is dragged outside the city to be stoned; and, finally, the scene of the stoning: St. Sthepen falls to his knees with his eyes raised to the vision of the Heavenly Kingdom.

In the lower portion we see at first the Pope St. Sixtus, with the features of Nicholas V, offering to St. Lawrence the chalice and the paten; in the following scene, the same Pope entrusts the Saint with the treasures of the Church, so that he may sell them and distribute the proceeds to the poor; on the left, two guards spy on the Pope and his minister. On the wall facing the altar, St. Lawrence stands on the threshold of an imposing temple with a rich perspective of columns: he is surrounded by a crowd of poor people with children, among them a lame man stretching out his hand; next comes the judgment of the Saint before the Emperor who tries in vain to intimidate him by showing whips and other instruments of torture; finally, on the third wall, we find St. Lawrence lying flat on his back on the grate, the executioners feeding the flames while protecting their faces with their hands, and the Emperor looking on from the top of a balustrade.

In these well preserved frescoes, on which Benozzo Gozzoli also worked as an assistant, the purest representative of the Renaissance has left insuperable proofs of his mystic fervor and the maturity of his art. Perhaps the greatest of Angelico's works, these frescoes were among his last, for he died almost at the same time as his great protector, in 1455, and was buried in the temple of Minerva in Rome.

Beato Angelico: *Martyrdom of St. Lawrence* (detail) - Beato Angélico: *Martirio de San Lorenzo* (detalle)
Fra Angelico: *Martyre de Saint Laurent* (détail) - Beato Angelico: *Martirio di S. Lorenzo* (particolare)

La primera en órden cronológico de las capillas conservadas hasta nuestros dias es la pintada por el Beato Angélico bajo Nicolas V, entre 1448 y 1450, mientras que la pintada para Eugenio IV entre 1445 y 1447 fué derribada en la construcción de la Sala Regia. Originariamente no era esta una capilla, sino un cuarto de trabajo o escritorio que el gran Pontífice humanista mandara sacar para sí de una torre del palacio de Nicolas III, incorporada con el nuevo edificio encargado por él para ofrecer a los Papas una morada más ancha y más decorosa. Con esta su primitiva destinación no contrastan las pinturas de sujeto religioso, pués estas, en aquellos tiempos, aplicábanse también a los locales de carácter profano. En este caso, además, son ellas completamente justificadas por ser San Lorenzo venerado como protector de los archivos y de las bibliotecas; por consiguiente, también el protomartir San Esteban le quedava asociado en la función y en culto eclesiástico, y era pués natural que la vida de lor dos Diáconos estuviera representada en dos zonas paralelas sobre tres de las paredes de la capilla, siendo la tercera ocupada por el altar y una gran ventana. En los triángulos del intradós de la bóveda estan pintados los Evangelistas con sus símbolos, y sobre los nichos de las paredes, los Doctores de la Iglesia.

En la zona superior, delimitada por los arcos de la bóveda, están representados episodios de la vida de San Esteban. De la izquierda a la derecha, las escenas son las siguientes: San Pedro que confiere al Santo el diaconado entregándole el cáliz; San Esteban que distribuye la limosna a los pobres; el Santo que discute publicamente con los Judíos; San Esteban delante del Tribunal del Sinedrio que lo está condenando a muerte;

Beato Angelico: *St. Lawrence Preaching* (detail) - Beato Angélico: *Predicación de San Lorenzo* (detalle)
Fra Angelico: *Predication de Saint Laurent* (détail) - Beato Angelico: *Predicazione di S. Lorenzo* (particolare)

el Santo arrastrando fuera de las murallas de la ciudad para ser lapidado; los apedreadores que rivalizan el herirlo, mientras el Santo échase de rodillos, con lo ojos levantados hacia el cielo, donde se le abre la visión de su patria celeste.

En la zona inferior vese primeramente el Santo Pontífice Sixto, con el semblante de Nicolas V, que ofrece a San Lorenzo el cáliz y la patena; en la escena siguiente el mismo Pontífice confía al Santo los tesoros de la Iglesia para vender a fin de distribuir el dinero a los pobres, mientras que, a la izquierda, dos sicarios espian a la acción del Papa y de su ministro. San Lorenzo reaparece sobre la pared enfrente del altar, en el umbral de un templo donde sobresale la rica perspectiva de las columnas: el Santo está rodeado por una muchedumbre de pobres con niños y hay también un tullido que tiende su mano. Sigue el juicio del Santo delante del Emperador que trada en balde amedrentarlo enseñándole los azotes y demás instrumentos de tortura. La escena está completada por el fresco de la tercera pared, donde se ve el Santo que esta echado supino sobre la parrilla, con los verdugos que alimentan a las llamas amparándose la cara, y el Emperador que asiste encima de una balaustrada. En estes frescos, a que trabajó también, como ayudante, Benozzo Gózzoli y que se hallan en estado de buena conservación, el más puro representante del Renacimiento dejó pruebas insuperables del místico fervor que lo inspiraba y de la madurez de su arte. Fué esta una de las últimas, y talvez la más importante, de las obras salidas de su pincel, pués murió él casi contemporaneamente a su gran protector en 1455, siendo sepultado en el templo de Minerva, en Roma.

Beato Angelico: *St. Lawrence Preaching* (detail) - Beato Angélico: *Predicación de San Lorenzo* (detalle)
Fra Angelico: *Prédication de saint Laurent* (détail) - Beato Angelico: *Predicazione di S. Lorenzo* (particolare)

La première par ordre chronologique et conservée jusqu'à nous, est la chapelle qui fut peinte par Fra Angelico sous Nicolas V entre les années 1448-1450; une autre, peinte pour Eugène IV entre 1445 et 1447, fut détruite lors de la construction de la Salle Royale. A l'origine il s'agissait non d'une chapelle mais d'une salle d'études ou cabinet de travail que le grand Pontife humaniste avait fait pratiquer dans une tour du palais de Nicolas III, incorporée au nouvel édifice érigé par lui pour en faire une habitation plus vaste et plus digne destinée aux Papes. Les peintures à sujets religieux que l'on appliquait en ce temps là communément même aux locaux d'usage profane n'étaient pas en contradiction avec la destination primitive du local. En ce cas particulier, elles sont d'ailleurs pleinement justifiées par le fait que diacre saint Laurent était vénéré comme protecteur des archives et des bibliothèques. Il en résultait que le premier martyr saint Etienne lui était associé dans cette fonction et dans le culte ecclésiastique, et que la vie des deux diacres était représentée en deux zones parallèles sur trois murs de la chapelle; le quatrième étant occupé par l'autel et par une grande fenêtre.
Sur les quatre quartiers de la voûte sont peints les Evangélistes avec leurs symboles, et dans les niches figurées sur les murs au dessous les Docteurs de l'Eglise.
Dans la zone supérieure encadrée par les arches de la voûte il y a les épisodes de la vie de saint Etienne. A partir de la gauche en allant vers la droite, on voit saint Pierre qui lui confère le diaconat en lui remettant le calice, puis saint Etienne distribuant l'aumône aux pauvres; sur le mur suivant, tout d'abord le saint qui discute publiquement avec les Juifs, tandis que sur la droite, en lieu clos, il est devant le tribunal du sanhédrin

Beato Angelico: *Martyrdom of St. Stephen* (detail) - Beato Angélico: *Martirio de San Esteban* (detalle)
Fra Angelico: *Martyre de saint Etienne* (détail) - Beato Angelico: *Martirio di S. Stefano* (particolare)

qui prononce contre lui la sentence de mort. Sur le troisième mur, saint Etienne est
entraîné hors des murs de la ville pour être lapidé; puis c'est entre les lapidateurs à qui
le frappera, et il tombe à genoux le regard levé au ciel où s'ouvre pour lui la patrie céleste.
Dans la zone inférieure on voit d'abord saint Sixte pape, sous les traits de Nicolas V,
qui présente au saint le calice et la patène; dans la scène suivante le même pontife
confie au saint les trésors de l'Eglise pour qu'il les vende et distribue l'argent aux
pauvres, tandis qu'à gauche deux sbires épient l'action du pape et de son ministre.
saint Laurent reparaît sur le mur en face de l'autel au seuil d'un temple imposant par
la riche perspective de ses colonnes: il est entouré d'une foule de pauvres avec des
enfants et un estropié qui tend la main. Vient ensuite le jugement du saint par devant
l'empereur qui essaie en vain de l'intimider en lui montrant les fouets et autres instruments du supplice. La scène continue et son épilogue est retracé dans la fresque du
troisième mur où le saint gît couché sur le gril; les bourreaux alimentent la flamme
en se protégeant le visage de leurs mains, et l'empereur assiste à la scène du haut
d'une balustrade. En ces fresques, auxquelles Benozzo Gozzoli aussi a collaboré comme
aide et qui sont bien conservées, le plus pur représentant de la Renaissance a légué
des preuves incomparables de la mystique ferveur de son inspiration et de la maturité
de son art. Ce fut une des dernières œuvres sorties de son pinceau, et peut-être la
plus considérable, car il mourut à peu près en même temps que son grand protecteur
en 1455 et fut enseveli dans l'Eglise de la Minerve à Rome.

90

Beato Angelico: *Martyrdom of St. Stephen* (detail) - Beato Angélico: *Martirio de San Esteban* (detalle)
Fra Angelico: *Martyre de saint Etienne* (détail) - Beato Angelico: *Martirio di S. Stefano* (particolare)

Prima in ordine cronologico e conservatasi fino a noi, è la Cappella affrescata dal Beato Angelico sotto Niccolò V fra gli anni 1448-1450, mentre quella dipinta per Eugenio IV tra il 1445-1447 andò distrutta nella costruzione della Sala Regia. Si trattava in origine non di una cappella, ma di una stanza di lavoro o di uno studio che il grande pontefice umanista aveva fatto ricavare per sè da una torre del palazzo di Niccolò III, incorporata col nuovo edificio eretto da lui per una più vasta e decorosa abitazione dei Papi. Con questa primitiva destinazione non contrastano le pitture di soggetto religioso che in quei tempi si applicavano comunemente anche ai locali d'uso profano. Nel caso particolare poi esse sono pienamente giustificate dal fatto che S. Lorenzo, quale Diacono, era venerato come protettore degli archivi e delle biblioteche. Ne veniva di conseguenza che anche il protomartire S. Stefano fosse associato a lui nella funzione e nel culto ecclesiastico, e che la vita dei due diaconi fosse rappresentata in due zone parallele su tre pareti della cappella: la quarta è occupata dall'altare e da una grande finestra.
Sui quattro spicchi della volta sono dipinti gli Evangelisti coi loro simboli, e sulle nicchie figurate nelle pareti sottostanti i Dottori della Chiesa.
Nella zona superiore incorniciata dagli archi della volta sono gli episodi della vita di S. Stefano. Cominciando da sinistra e proseguendo a destra: quando S. Pietro gli conferisce il diaconato consegnandogli il calice, poi S. Stefano quando distribuisce l'elemosina ai poveri; sulla parete seguente si vede prima il Santo discutere pubblicamente con gli Ebrei, mentre più a destra in luogo chiuso egli si trova dinanzi al tribunale del Sine-

Beato Angelico: *Martyrdom of St. Stephen* (detail) - Beato Angélico: *Martirio de San Esteban* (detalle)
Fra Angelico: *Martyre de saint Etienne* (détail) - Beato Angelico: *Martirio di S. Stefano* (particolare)

drio che pronuncia contro di lui la sentenza di morte; sulla terza parete S. Stefano è
trascinato fuori le mura della città per essere lapidato: quindi i lapidatori fanno a gara
per colpirlo ed egli cade genuflesso con lo sguardo rivolto al cielo, dove gli si dischiude
la patria celeste.
Nella zona inferiore si vede da principio il Santo Pontefice Sisto, coi lineamenti di
Niccolò V, che porge a S. Lorenzo il calice e la patena; nella scena seguente il Pontefice
medesimo affida al Santo i tesori della chiesa da vendere per distribuire il denaro ai
poveri, mentre a sinistra due sgherri spiano l'azione del Papa e del suo ministro.
S. Lorenzo riappare nella parete di fronte all'altare sulla soglia di un tempio che s'impone
per la ricca prospettiva delle colonne: lo circonda una folla di poveri con bambini ed
uno storpio nel mezzo che tende la mano. Viene in seguito il giudizio del Santo dinanzi
all'imperatore che tenta invano d'intimidirlo mostrandogli i flagelli e gli altri strumenti del martirio. La scena continua ed ha il suo epilogo nell'affresco della terza parete,
dove il Santo giace supino sulla graticola, i carnefici alimentano le fiamme riparandosi
il volto con le mani, e l'imperatore assiste dall'alto di una balaustrata. In questi affreschi, in cui ha lavorato come aiuto anche Benozzo Gozzoli e che sono in uno stato di
buona conservazione, il più puro rappresentante del Rinascimento ha lasciato insupe-
rabili prove del mistico fervore da cui era ispirato e della maturità dell'arte sua. Fu
una delle ultime, e forse la maggiore, delle opere uscite dal suo pennello, perchè morì
quasi contemporaneamente al suo grande protettore nel 1455 e fu sepolto nel tempio
della Minerva in Roma.

92

Beato Angelico: *The Pope Entrusting St. Lawrence with the Treasures of the Church*
Beato Angélico: *El Papa entrega a San Lorenzo los tesoros de la Iglesia*
Fra Angelico: *Le Pape remet à saint Laurent les trésors de l'Eglise*
Beato Angelico: *Il Papa consegna a S. Lorenzo i tesori della Chiesa*

Beato Angelico: *The Pope Entrusting St. Lawrence with the Treasures of the Church* (detail)
Beato Angélico: *El Papa entrega a San Lorenzo los tesoros de la Iglesia* (detalle)
Fra Angelico: *Le Pape remet à saint Laurent les trésors de l'Eglise* (détail)
Beato Angelico: *Il Papa consegna a S. Lorenzo i tesori della Chiesa* (particolare)

94

Beato Angelico: *St. Lawrence Giving Alms* - Beato Angélico: *San Lorenzo distribuye las limosnas*
Fra Angelico: *Saint Laurent distribuant les aumônes* - Beato Angelico: *S. Lorenzo distribuisce le elemosine*

95

Beato Angelico: *St. Lawrence Giving Alms* (detail)
Beato Angélico: *San Lorenzo distribuye las limosnas* (detalle)
Fra Angelico: *Saint Laurent distribuant les aumônes* (détail)
Beato Angelico: *S. Lorenzo distribuisce le elemosine* (particolare)

THE SISTINE CHAPEL

LA CAPILLA SIXTINA

LA CHAPELLE SIXTINE

LA CAPPELLA SISTINA

View of the interior of the Sistine Chapel - Vista interior de la Capilla Sixtina
Vue intérieure de la Chapelle Sixtine - Veduta interna della Cappella Sistina

Choir of the Sistine Chapel - Coro de la Capilla Sixtina
Tribune des chantres de la Chapelle Sixtine - Cantoria della Cappella Sistina

Railing of the Sistine Chapel - Verja de la Capilla Sixtina
Grille de la Chapelle Sixtine - Cancellata della Cappella Sistina

100

Michelangelo: *The Creation of Man* (detail) - Miguel Ángel: *Creación del Hombre* (detalle)
Michel-Ange: *Création de l'homme* (détail) - Michelangelo: *Creazione dell'uomo* (particolare)

This is the most famous building of the Palace and here, since Paul III, have been held the conclaves for the election of the Popes. The frescoes on its walls offer for the admiration of the world the most sublime creations of Italian Renaissance painting. The order to build the Chapel was given to the Florentine Giovannino de' Dolci by Sixtus IV (1471-1484), and work was begun in 1473. The wall frescoes were painted during the years 1481-1483, so that in August, 1484, the Pope was able to dedicate it with great solemnity to the Virgin. Not unworthy of these famous paintings are the very delicate marble reliefs of the Choir and the Railing, executed by Mino Da Fiesole, Giovanni Dalmata and Andrea Bregno (page 100). The artists who did the pictorial work over a period of fifty years took for their theme the history of mankind, from the beginning of the world to the Last Judgment, through all its significant phases: the Creation, the Original Sin and the Flood, on the ceiling; the Deliverance of the Jews from captivity in Egypt, on the left wall (as you look toward the altar); the Redemption of mankind from sin through the intervention of Christ, on the opposite wall; the Last Judgment, portraying the inescapable destiny of man, on the back wall behind the altar.

Many great Umbro-Tuscan masters of the second half of the fifteenth century vied with each other in painting the frescoes of the side walls: Perugino, Pinturicchio, Botticelli, Cosimo Rosselli, Domenico Ghirlandaio, Luca Signorelli, Fra' Diamante. But they were all surpassed by Michelangelo who did all by himself the ceiling and

Michelangelo: *The Creation of Woman* - Miguel Ángel : *Creación de la mujer*
Michel-Ange: *Création de la femme* - Michelangelo: *Creazione della donna*

the back wall in two different periods. From 1508 to 1512 he painted on the immense ceiling a series of frescoes in which more than 340 figures come to life, among them the imposing Prophets and Sibyls (see the figures of Jeremiah, and the Erythraean and Delphic Sibyls). Twenty-four years later he covered the back wall with the awesome visions of the Last Judgment, where throng, shaken by terror or exalted by hope, the souls of the elect and the damned, angels and demons: altogether 391 figures. Among these may be seen the distorted face of Michelangelo himself, painted on the tattered skin held by the Apostle St. Bartholomew, and the profile of Dante, in a group of the elect, to the right of the Judging Christ (page 107).

In developing this great theme Michelangelo could not ignore the examples of his predecessors, but in the execution of the idea he freed himself completely and attained an originality which admits neither comparison nor imitation.

Michelangelo: *The Drunkennes of Noah* - Miguel Ángel: *Embriaguez de Noé*
Michel-Ange: *Ivresse de Noë* - Michelangelo: *Ebbrezza di Noè*

Es el edificio sacro y artístico más afamado del Palacio, donde se hacen normalmente los conclaves para la elección de los Papas, y donde, en los frescos que recubren sus paredes, ofrécense a la admiración del mundo las más sublimes creaciones de la pintura italiana del Renacimiento. Encargada por Sixto IV (1471-1484) al florentino Giovannino de' Dolci, su construcción fué empezada en 1473. En el período de 1481 a 1484 ejecutáronse los frescos de las paredes, de manera que en agosto de 1484 el Pontífice pudo dedicarla solemnemente a la Asunción. Hacen digna corona a la decoración pintada los delicadísimos relieves marmóreos del coro y de la verja, donde trabajaron juntos Mino da Fiésole, Giovanni Dálmata y Andrea Bregno (pág. 100). El asunto ilustrado en la decoración, que fué completada en un período de cincuenta años, fué la historia de la humanidad, desde la creación del mundo hasta al juicio universal, representada en sus fases más importantes: la creación, el pecado original y el diluvio en la bóveda; la liberación de los Judios de la esclavitud de Egipto bajo la guia de Moisés en la pared izquierda, mirando hacia el altar; la liberación de la humanidad de la esclavitud del pecado, cumplida por Jesucristo, en la pared derecha, y el juicio universal en la pared de fondo, que domina el altar.

En los frescos de las paredes laterales rivalizaron los maestros umbro-tuscanos de la segunda mitad de 1400: el Perugino, el Pinturicchio, Botticelli, Cósimo Rosselli, Doménico Ghirlandaio, Luca Signorelli y Fra Diamante, pero a todos les sobrepujó Miguel Ángel que, solo, pintó en un primer período (1508 a 1512) la inmensa bóveda

103

Michelangelo: *The Expulsion of Adam and Eve from the Garden of Eden* (detail)
Miguel Ángel: *Adán y Eva cazados del Paraíso* (detalle)
Michel-Ange: *Adam et Ève chassés du Paradis terrestre* (détail)
Michelangelo: *Cacciata di Adamo ed Eva dal Paradiso terrestre* (particolare)

con un ciclo de frescos que incluyen más que 340 figuras, con las gigantescas de los Profetas y de las Sibilas (véanse las figuras de Jeremía y de las Sibilas Eritrea y Délfica), mientras que, en un período sucesivo — veintecuatro años después — recubrió con las terribles visiones del juicio la pared de fondo, donde agólpanse, turbadas por el terror o aliviadas por la esperanza, ánimas electas, ánimas condenadas, ángeles y demonios, con un total de 391 figuras. Ni faltan entre estas la cara desfigurada de Miguel Ángel en la piel del Apostol San Bartolomeo, y el perfil de Dante que está en un grupo de electos en lo alto, a la derecha del Cristo juzgante (pág. 107). Aún, en desarrollar el asunto que le había sido propuesto, Miguel Ángel no pudo ignorar a los ejemplos de sus precursores, en la actuación de la idea se desapegó él completamente de ellos, dejando en su obra los señales de una originalidad que no permite ninguna comparación o imitación.

Michelangelo: *The Flood* (detail) - Miguel Ángel: *Diluvio Universal* (detalle)
Michel-Ange: *Déluge Universel* (détail) - Michelangelo: *Diluvio Universale* (particolare)

C'est l'édifice religieux et artistique le plus fameux du Palais où, à partir de Paul III, se sont tenus régulièrement les conclaves pour l'élection des Papes, et dans lequel, grâce aux fresques dont les murs sont revêtus, s'offrent à l'admiration du monde les plus sublimes créations de la peinture italienne de la Renaissance. Commandée par Sixte IV (1471-1484) au Florentin Giovannino de' Dolci, celui-ci en commença la construction en 1473. Durant les années 1481-1483 furent exécutées les fresques des murs, si bien qu'en août 1484 le Souverain Pontife put en faire la dédicace solennelle à l'Assomption. Un digne couronnement de la décoration peinte est constitué par les reliefs si délicats de la tribune des Chantres et de la grille auxquels travaillèrent à la fois Mino da Fiesole, Giovanni Dalmata et Andrea Bregno (page 100). Le sujet illustré par les artistes dans la décoration peinte, qui se déroule sur une période de cinquante années, fut l'histoire de l'humanité, depuis la création du monde jusqu'au Jugement dernier, représentée dans ses phases prédominantes: la création, le péché originel et le déluge sur la voûte; la libération des Hébreux de leur captivité en Egypte sous la conduite de Moïse sur le mur à gauche en regardant l'autel; la libération de l'humanité par le Christ qui l'arrache à l'esclavage du péché, sur la muraille opposée à droite; le jugement dernier qui fixe les immuables destins de l'homme sur le mur du fond dominant l'autel.

Dans les fresques des murs latéraux les maîtres umbro-toscans de la seconde moitié du Quattrocento rivalisèrent entre eux: le Pérugin, le Pinturicchio, Botticelli, Cosimo Rosselli, Domenico Ghirlandajo, Luca Signorelli, Fra Diamante, mais Michel-Ange

Michelangelo: *The Last Judgment* (detail) - Miguel Ángel: *Juicio Universal* (detalle)
Michel-Ange: *Jugement dernier* (détail) - Michelangelo: *Giudizio Universale* (particolare)

les a tous surpassés à lui seul, et à deux reprises : la première fois (de 1508 à 1512) en peignant l'immense voûte avec un ciel de fresques dans lesquelles revivent plus de 340 figures, entre autres celles des gigantesques Prophètes et Sibylles (v. les figures de Jérémie et des Sibylles d'Erythrée et de Delphes); la seconde (vingt-quatre ans après) quand il recouvrit avec les terribles visions du jugement le mur du fond, où se pressent, agitées par la terreur et soulevées par l'espérance, âmes élues, âmes damnées, anges et démons, en tout 391 figures. Parmi celles-ci le visage défiguré de Michel-Ange est présent sous les traits de l'apôtre saint Barthélemy, de même que le profil de Dante qui se trouve dans un groupe d'élus en haut, à la droite du Christ venu pour juger (page 107).

En développant le sujet qu'il s'était proposé, Michel-Ange ne pouvait ignorer les exemples de ses prédécesseurs, mais au cours de l'exécution il s'en est complètement détaché, ce qui fait que son œuvre est empreinte d'un caractère d'originalité incomparable et propre à décourager tous les imitateurs.

Michelangelo: *A Group of the Elects* (detail of the « Last Judgment »)
Miguel Ángel: *Un grupo de electos* («Juicio Universal», detalle)
Michel-Ange: *Groupe d'élus* (détail du « Jugement dernier »)
Michelangelo: *Un gruppo di eletti* (particolare del « Giudizio Universale »)

E' l'edificio sacro ed artistico più famoso del Palazzo, dove, da Paolo III in poi, si tengono di regola i conclavi per l'elezione dei Papi, e nella quale, con gli affreschi che rivestono le pareti, si offrono all'ammirazione del mondo le più sublimi creazioni della pittura italiana del Rinascimento. Ordinata da Sisto IV (1471-1484) al fiorentino Giovannino de' Dolci, questi ne cominciò la costruzione nel 1473. Negli anni 1481-1483 furono eseguiti gli affreschi delle pareti, cosicchè nell'agosto del 1484 il Pontefice potè farne la dedicazione solenne all'Assunta. Fanno degna corona alla decorazione pittorica i delicatissimi rilievi marmorei della cantoria e della cancellata, a cui lavorarono insieme Mino da Fiesole, Giovanni Dalmata e Andrea Bregno (pag. 100). Il tema illustrato dagli artisti nella decorazione pittorica, che si svolge in un periodo di cinquant'anni, fu la storia dell'umanità, dalla creazione del mondo fino al giudizio universale, rappresentata nelle fasi predominanti: la creazione, il peccato originale e il diluvio nella volta; la liberazione degli Ebrei dalla schiavitù dell'Egitto sotto la guida di Mosè nella parete a sinistra di chi guarda l'altare; la liberazione dell'umanità dalla schiavitù del peccato, compiuta da Cristo, nella parete opposta a destra; il giudizio universale che segna gli immutabili destini dell'uomo nella parete di fondo che sovrasta l'altare.
Negli affreschi dei muri laterali gareggiarono tra loro i maestri umbro-toscani della seconda metà del '400: il Perugino, il Pinturicchio, il Botticelli, Cosimo Rosselli, Domenico Ghirlandaio, Luca Signorelli, Fra' Diamante, ma tutti li superò Miche-

107

Michelangelo: *Nude Torso* - Miguel Ángel: *Tronco de un desnudo*
Michel-Ange: *Torse nu* - Michelangelo: *Torso di un nudo*

langelo, che da solo, e in due riprese: la prima (dal 1508 al 1512) dipinse l'immensa volta con un ciclo di affreschi nei quali rivivono più di 340 figure, tra cui quelle gigantesche dei Profeti e delle Sibille (vedi le figure di Geremia e delle Sibille Eritrea e Delfica); la seconda (ventiquattro anni dopo), quando ricoprì con le terribili visioni del giudizio la parete di fondo, dove si affollano agitate dal terrore o sollevate dalla speranza anime elette, anime dannate, angeli e demoni: in tutto 391 figure. Non manca tra queste il volto sfigurato di Michelangelo nella pelle dell'Apostolo S. Bartolomeo, e il profilo di Dante che sta in un gruppo di eletti in alto alla destra del Cristo giudicante (pag. 107). Nello svolgere il tema che gli era stato proposto Michelangelo non poteva ignorare gli esempi dei suoi precursori, ma nell'attuazione dell'idea se n'è completamente distaccato ed ha impresso nell'opera i segni di un'originalità che non ammette nè confronti nè imitatori.

Michelangelo: *The Prophet Jeremiah* (detail) - Miguel Ángel: *El Profeta Jeremias* (detalle)
Michel-Ange: *Le prophète Jérémie* (détail) - Michelangelo: *Il Profeta Geremia* (particolare)

Michelangelo: *The Erythraean Sibyl* - Miguel Angel: *La Sibila Eritrea*
Michel-Ange: *La Sibylle d'Erythrée* - Michelangelo: *La Sibilla Eritrea*

Michelangelo: *The Delphic Sibyl* - Miguel Ángel: *La Sibila Delfica*
Michel-Ange: *La Sibylle de Delphes* - Michelangelo: *La Sibilla Delfica*

Michelangelo: *Head of Adam* (detail of the « Creation of Man »)
Miguel Ángel: *Cabeza de Adán* (detalle de la « Creación del hombre »)
Michel-Ange: *Tête d'Adam* (détail de la « Création de l'homme »)
Michelangelo: *Testa di Adamo* (particolare della « Creazione dell'uomo »)

Michelangelo: *Head of God the Father* (detail of the « Creation of Man »)
Miguel Ángel: *Cabeza del Padre Eterno* (detalle de la « Creación del hombre »)
Michel-Ange: *Tête du Père Eternel* (détail de la « Création de l'homme »)
Michelangelo: *Testa del Padre Eterno* (particolare della « Creazione dell'uomo »)

Michelangelo: *The Last Judgment* (view of the whole) - Miguel Ángel: *El Juicio Universal* (conjunto)
Michel-Ange: *Le Jugement dernier* (vue d'ensemble) - Michelangelo: *Il Giudizio Universale* (veduta d'assieme)

114

Michelangelo: *The Last Judgment* (Christ as Judge and the Blessed Virgin)
Miguel Ángel: *Juicio Universal* (el Cristo juzgante y la Beata Vírgen)
Michel-Ange: *Le Jugement dernier* (le Christ juge et la Sainte Vierge)
Michelangelo: *Il Giudizio Universale* (il Cristo giudicante e la Beata Vergine)

Michelangelo: *The Last Judgment* (detail) - Miguel Ángel: *Juicio Universal* (detalle)
Michel-Ange: *Le Jugement dernier* (détail) - Michelangelo: *Il Giudizio Universale* (particolare)

116

Michelangelo: *The Last Judgment* (St. Bartholomew) - Miguel Ángel: *Juicio Universal* (San Bartolomeo)
Michel-Ange: *Le Jugement dernier* (S. Barthélemy) - Michelangelo: *Il Giudizio Universale* (S. Bartolomeo)

117

Michelangelo: *The Last Judgment* (An Angel Driving one the Damned back into Hell)
Miguel Ángel: *Juicio Universal* (Un Ángel que rechaza un réprobo en el infierno)
Michel-Ange: *Le Jugement dernier* (Ange qui rejette un damné à l'enfer)
Michelangelo: *Il Giudizio Universale* (Un angelo che ricaccia un dannato nell' inferno)

Michelangelo: *The Last Judgment* (Angel with Rosary) - Miguel Ángel: *Juicio Universal* (Ángel con la corona del rosario)
Michel-Ange: *Le Jugement dernier* (Ange au rosaire) - Michelangelo: *Il Giudizio Universale* (Angelo con corona del rosario)

Michelangelo: *The Last Judgment* (detail of a Demon)
Miguel Ángel: *Juicio Universal* (detalle de un demonio)
Michel-Ange: *Le Jugement dernier* (détail d'un démon)
Michelangelo: *Il Giudizio Universale* (particolare di un demonio)

Michelangelo: *The Last Judgment* (detail of one of the Damned)
Miguel Ángel: *Juicio Universal* (detalle de un réprobo)
Michel-Ange: *Le Jugement dernier* (détail d'un damné)
Michelangelo: *Il Giudizio Universale* (particolare di un dannato)

121

Botticelli: *Moses and the Daughters of Jethro* - Botticelli: *Moisés y las hijas de Yetro*
Botticelli: *Moïse et les filles de Jethro* - Botticelli: *Mosè e le figlie di Jetro*

Botticelli: *The Leper's Sacrifice* - Botticelli: *El Sacrificio del leproso*
Botticelli: *Sacrifice du lépreux* - Botticelli: *Sacrificio del lebbroso*

Botticelli: *Moses and the Daughters of Jethro* (detail) - Botticelli: *Moisés y las hijas de Yetro* (detalle)
Botticelli: *Moïse et les filles de Jethro* (détail) - Botticelli: *Mosè e le figlie di Jetro* (particolare)

Ghirlandaio: *The Calling of the Apostles* - Ghirlandaio: *Vocación de los Apóstoles*
Ghirlandaio: *Vocation des Apôtres* - Ghirlandaio: *Vocazione degli Apostoli*

Botticelli: *The Temptation of Jesus* - Botticelli: *Las tentaciones de Jesucristo*
Botticelli: *Tentations de Jésus* - Botticelli: *Tentazioni di Gesù*

Ghirlandaio: *The Calling of the Apostles* (detail) - Ghirlandaio: *Vocación de los Apóstoles* (detalle)
Ghirlandaio: *Vocation des Apôtres* (détail) - Ghirlandaio: *Vocazione degli Apostoli* (particolare)

125

Perugino: *The Consignment of the Keys* - Perugino: *La entrega de las llaves*
Perugino: *La remise des clefs* - Perugino: *La consegna delle chiavi*

Botticelli: *Punishment by Divine Fire* - Botticelli: *El castigo del fuego celeste*
Botticelli: *Châtiment du feu divin* - Botticelli: *Castigo del fuoco celeste*

126

Perugino: *The Consignment of the Keys* (detail) - Perugino: *La entrega de las llaves* (detalle)
Perugino: *Le remise des clefs* (détail) - Perugino: *Consegna delle chiavi* (particolare)

Pinturicchio: *Circumcision of the Sons of Moses* - Pinturicchio: *Circuncisión de los hijos de Moisés*
Pinturicchio: *Circoncision des fils de Moïse* - Pinturicchio: *Circoncisione dei figli di Mosè*

Rosselli (?): *The Crossing of the Red Sea* - Rosselli (?): *El Pasaje del Mar Rojo*
Rosselli (?): *Passage de la Mer Rouge* - Rosselli (?): *Passaggio del Mar Rosso*

128

THE PAULINE CHAPEL

LA CAPILLA PAULINA

LA CHAPELLE PAULINE

LA CAPPELLA PAOLINA

Constructed by the younger Antonio da Sangallo for Paul III (1534-1549), the Pauline Chapel, despite its more modest proportions, ranks next in importance to the Sistine Chapel because of its historical values and as an expression of a new period in art. While painting reigns supreme in the Sistine Chapel, here architecture has also an important place, as shown by the beautiful reliefs of columns and moldings. These reliefs give movement to the masses and create a play of lights and shadows which anticipates the baroque. The Pauline Chapel honors with its name the Pope who ordered its construction, but its fame is due mostly to the great frescoes which cover its side walls, i. e. the scenes of the Conversion of Saul and the Crucifixion of St. Peter. These were Michelangelo's last paintings, and all his genius is there. Observe, in the Conversion of Saul, the sudden disappearance of all the people after the flash of lightning which makes the horse rear and flings from the saddle the persecutor who listens, blinded, to the voice of God calling him from Heaven. And observe, in the second fresco, the masses of soldiers and people milling around the cross implanted in the earth, and the Apostle who, resigned to his fate, watches impassive and serene the crowd surrounding him. On the right there is a tall, impressive figure of a man who stands with his hands crossed on his breast, meditating sorrowfully on the scene to which he is an unwilling witness. He seems to be repeating the sad saying in the liturgy: « See how the just man dies, and no one seems to realize it! ». It is possible that in this figure and his features Michelangelo wanted to leave a lasting memory of his own person.

Construida por Antonio de Sangallo el jóven por encargo de Pablo III (1543-1549) es de proporciones más reducidas que las de la Capilla Sixtina; a pesar de esto, la Capilla Paulina merece ocupar al lugar más próximo a la hermana mayor debido a su valor histórico y por la expresión de un nuevo período artístico. Mientras que en la Capilla Sixtina domina soberana la pintura, aquí la arquitectura toma un lugar sobresaliente y afírmase esplendidamente con relieves de columnas, cornisas y estucos que dan movimiento a las masas y crean juegos de sombras y de luces que ya preludian el barroco. El nombre de la Capilla recuerda el pontífice que la mandó edificar, pero en los frescos principales que cubren a las paredes laterales sobresalen las dos escenas de la conversión de Saul y de la crucifixión de San Pedro, donde Miguel Ángel escribió su testamento de pintor, y ¡ que pintor ! Véase en la conversión de Saul el repentino dispersarse de todos los personajes al estallido del rayo que hace encabritarse el caballo y apear el persecutor que, cegado, escucha desde el cielo la voz de Diós que lo llama. Y véase también en el segundo fresco, del otro lado, el rodear de las masas de soldados y de gentío alrededor de la cruz plantada en el terreno y del Apóstol que, ya resignado a su destino, mira impasible y sereno a la muchedumbre que lo rodea. Hace impresión la alta figura de un personaje, de pié y con los brazos cruzados sobre el pecho, que medita tristemente sobre lo que esta mirando mal de su grado, y parece repertir el dicho desconsolado de la liturgía: « Mire al hombre justo que se muere, y nadie hace caso ! ». Y no parece imposible que en esta figura y en sus rasgos Miguel Ángel quizera dejar un recuerdo de su propia persona.

Construite par Antonio da Sangallo le jeune, répondant à la volonté de Paul III (1534-1549), et de proportions plus modestes que la Sixtine, elle mérite néanmoins d'occuper la place la plus voisine auprès de sa grande sœur, et pour sa valeur historique et comme expression d'une période artistique nouvelle. Tandis que la peinture domine souveraine dans la Chapelle Sixtine, l'architecture ici prend une place distincte et s'affirme en toute sa splendeur avec des reliefs de colonnes, de corniches et de stucs qui donnent du mouvement aux masses et créent des jeux d'ombres et de lumières qui préludent au baroque. Elle rappelle par son nom le pontife qui l'a voulue, mais dans les fresques principales qui revêtent les murs latéraux ce qui frappe le regard ce sont les deux scènes de la conversion de Saul et de la crucifixion de saint Pierre, où Michel-Ange a écrit son testament de peintre, et quel peintre ! Il faut voir dans la conversion de Saul la dispersion soudaine de tous les personnages sous la foudre qui fait cabrer le cheval et désarçonne le persécuteur tandis qu'il écoute, aveuglé, venant du ciel la voix de Dieu qui le rappelle. Et il faut voir encore, dans la seconde fresque, de l'autre côté, les soldats et le peuple massés en cercle autour de la croix déjà plantée et de l'apôtre qui, résigné à son destin, regarde impassible et serein la foule qui l'environne. Une haute figure, à droite, fait impression: celle d'un personnage debout, les mains croisées sur la poitrine, qui médite tristement sur l'action à laquelle il assiste malgré lui et semble répéter le mot désolé de la liturgie: « Vois comme le juste meurt, et chacun fait la sourde oreille ! ». On ne s'écarte pas de la vérité si l'on suppose que dans cette figure et sous ces traits Michel-Ange aura voulu laisser en souvenir l'image de sa personne.

Costruita da Antonio da Sangallo il giovane per volontà di Paolo III (1543-1549), e di proporzioni più modeste della Sistina, essa merita tuttavia di occupare il posto più vicino alla sorella maggiore, per i suoi pregi storici e come espressione di un nuovo periodo artistico. Mentre nella Cappella Sistina domina sovrana la pittura, qui l'architettura prende un posto distinto e si afferma splendidamente con rilievi di colonne, di cornici e di stucchi, che danno movimento alle masse e creano giuochi d'ombra e di luce che preludono al barocco. Essa ricorda col suo nome il pontefice che l'ha voluta, ma negli affreschi principali che rivestono le pareti laterali, colpiscono l'occhio le due scene della conversione di Saulo e della crocefissione di S. Pietro, in cui Michelangelo ha scritto il suo testamento di pittore, e quale pittore ! Vedasi nella conversione di Saulo il subitaneo disperdersi di tutti i personaggi allo scoppio del fulmine che fa impennare il cavallo e sbalza di sella il persecutore, il quale, accecato, ascolta dal cielo la voce di Dio che lo richiama. E vedasi nella seconda, dall'altro lato, il roteare delle masse di soldati e di popolo intorno alla croce piantata nel terreno e all'Apostolo che, rassegnato al suo destino, guarda impassibile e sereno la turba che lo circonda. Fa impressione l'alta figura a destra di un personaggio ritto con le mani incrociate sul petto, che medita tristamente sul fatto a cui assiste suo malgrado e pare ripetere il detto sconsolato della liturgia: « Vedi come l'uomo giusto muore, e nessuno se ne dà per inteso ! ». Non è fuor del vero pensare che in questa figura e nelle sue fattezze Michelangelo abbia voluto lasciare un ricordo della sua persona.

Michelangelo: *The Fall of St. Paul* - Miguel Ángel: *La caída de San Pablo*
Michel-Ange: *Chute de saint Paul* - Michelangelo: *Caduta di S. Paolo*

Michelangelo: *The Crucifixion of St. Peter* - Miguel Ángel: *Crucifixión de San Pedro*
Michel-Ange: *Crucifixion de saint Pierre* - Michelangelo: *Crocefissione di S. Pietro*

Michelangelo: *The Fall of St. Paul* (detail) - Miguel Ángel: *La caída de San Pablo* (detalle)
Michel-Ange: *Chute de saint Paul* (détail) - Michelangelo: *Caduta di S. Paolo* (particolare)

Michelangelo: *The Fall of St. Paul* (detail) - Miguel Ángel: *La caída de San Pablo* (detalle)
Michel-Ange: *Chute de saint Paul* (détail) - Michelangelo: *Caduta di S. Paolo* (particolare)

136

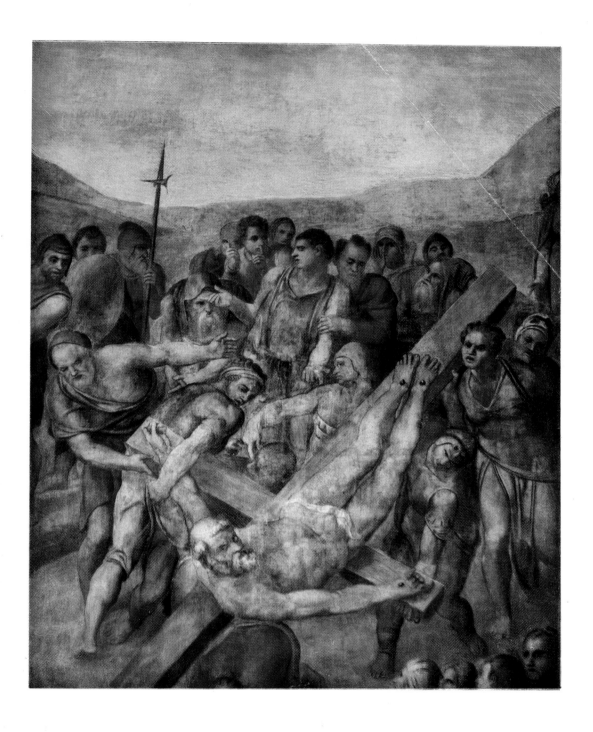

Michelangelo: *The Crucifixion of St. Peter* (detail) - Miguel Ángel: *Crucifixión de San Pedro* (detalle)
Michel-Ange: *Crucifixion de saint Pierre* (détail) - Michelangelo: *Crocefissione di S. Pietro* (particolare)

Michelangelo: *The Crucifixion of St. Peter* (detail) - Miguel Ángel: *Crucifixión de San Pedro* (detalle)
Michel-Ange: *Crucifixion de saint Pierre* (détail) - Michelangelo: *Crocefissione di S. Pietro* (particolare)

Michelangelo: *The Crucifixion of St. Peter* (detail) - Miguel Ángel: *Crucifixión de San Pedro* (detalle)
Michel-Ange: *Crucifixion de saint Pierre* (détail) - Michelangelo: *Crocefissione di S. Pietro* (particolare)

Michelangelo: *The Crucifixion of St. Peter* (detail) - Miguel Ángel: *Crucifixión de San Pedro* (detalle)
Michel-Ange: *Crucifixion de saint Pierre* (détail) - Michelangelo: *Crocefissione di S. Pietro* (particolare)

Michelangelo: *The Crucifixion of St. Peter* (detail) - Miguel Ángel: *Crucifixión de San Pedro* (detalle)
Michel-Ange: *Crucifixion de saint Pierre* (détail) - Michelangelo: *Crocefissione di S. Pietro* (particolare)

THE BORGIA APARTMENT

EL APOSENTO BORJA

L'APPARTEMENT DES BORGIA

L'APPARTAMENTO BORGIA

Pinturicchio: *Two Hermits in the Desert* - Pinturicchio: *Dos Hermitaños en el desierto*
Pinturicchio: *Deux ermites au désert* - Pinturicchio: *Due eremiti nel deserto*

The Borgia Apartment, on the first floor of the Palace of Nicholas V, toward the Belvedere Court, owes its name and its fame to Alexander VI: besides adding a tower to it, he had it decorated with frescoes by the Umbrian artist, Bernardino di Betto, called Pinturicchio, who worked there with his assistants from 1492 to 1495. It has six halls. However, the largest of them, called the Hall of the Popes, has no trace left of Pinturicchio, as the wooden ceiling collapsed in 1500 and was replaced by a vaulted one under Leo X who had it painted by Pierin del Vaga and Giovanni da Udine. In the four corners of this Hall we see large trophies with the coat of arms of the Medicis; and emblems alluding to the Medici family may also be seen in the central *tondo* with the dancing fawns. In the quadrangular sections which surround the central *tondo* and in the oval frescoes lying underneath are depicted the Signs of the Zodiac and the major planets and constellations. Hanging on the walls are six Flemish tapestries of the sixteenth century with episodes from the legend of Cephalus and Procris. In the other halls we admire tapestries of smaller size, but of equal beauty: one of these represents the Marriage of St. Catherine, another the picture by Raphael called « Lo spasimo ». But the most important halls, resplendent with the art of the Umbrian painter, are the there smaller ones which precede the Hall of the Popes, i. e. the Hall of the Mysteries, the Hall of the Saints and the Hall of the Liberal Arts.
The Hall of the Mysteries contains some of the greatest Umbrian masterpieces of the fifteenth century, filled with religious feeling, simplicity and grace. The frescoes of

143

Pinturicchio: *Group of Musicians* - Pinturicchio: *Grupo de músicos*
Pinturicchio: *Groupe de musiciens* - Pinturicchio: *Gruppo di musicanti*

the Annunciation and the Nativity are particularly admirable, and even more significant, in the fresco of the Resurrection, is the figure of Alexander VI kneeling in prayer:
it is one of the most marvellous historical portraits of the Renaissance, comparable
to that of Sixtus IV by Melozzo da Forlì.

A *tondo* over the door between the Hall of the Saints and the Hall of the Mysteries
shows the Virgin holding an open book, while the Holy Child, standing on a cushion,
appears to be reading. This fresco is reproduced in the frontispiece of this volume.
In the Hall of the Saints, where events from the lives of the Saints are reproduced,
Pinturicchio's art reaches real perfection through the liveliness of the composition and
the splendor of the coloring: see, for instance, the Dispute of St. Catherine, and the
picture of a gay party returning from a hunt on the Roman plains. Also noteworthy
is a scene from the life of the anchorites in the desert, in which temptation is represented by a group of maidens with bat-like wings and horns showing in their hair. And we
must mention the frescoes of the Visitation, with some spinners at work in a household
interior, and of St. Barbara fleeing from her father; finally, the fresco of St. Sebastian,
with the Coliseum and the Church of St. John and St. Paul visible in the background.
The Hall of the Liberal Arts, which comes after the Hall of the Saints, contains the
remarkable fresco of Music, in which the Queen of Harmony sits on a throne, surrounded by a chorus of musicians.

Pinturicchio: *The Visitation* - Pinturicchio: *La Visitación*
Pinturicchio: *La Visitation* - Pinturicchio: *La Visitazione*

El aposento Borja, al primer piso del Palacio de Nicolas V hacia el gran patio de Belvedere, debe su nombre y su fama a Alejandro VI que le añadió la torre que lleva su nombre y encargó su decoración con frescos al pintor umbro Bernardino de Betto, dicho el Pinturicchio, que trabajó a esta obra con sus ayudantes de 1492 a 1495. El aposento compónese de 6 salas. La más grande, dicha de los Pontífices, no tiene traza de la mano de Pinturicchio: el techo de madera caió en 1500 y fué reedificado en bóveda bajo León X que lo mandó pintar por Pierin del Vaga y Giovanni de Udine. En los cuatro cantos hay grandes troféos con armas medíceas, y tambien en círculo central hay faunos con insignias que aluden a la familia de los Médicis. En las zonas cuadrangulares que encierran al círculo central, y en los ovalos más abajo, están representados los signos zodiacales y unas constelaciones. Colgados a las paredes admíranse aquí 6 tapices de arte flamenca de 1500 que reproducen a la leyenda de Cefalo y Procri. En las demás salas hay más tapices de dimensiones menores pero de calidad finísima: uno de ellos representa a las nupcias de Santa Catalina, otro el cuadro de Rafael conocido con el título de « Angustia de Sicilia ». Pero las salas principales, donde resplendece de manera insuperable el arte del maestro umbro son las tres menores que preceden la de los Pontífices, eso es la sala de los Misterios, la Sala de los Santos y la Sala de las Artes Liberales.
La Sala de los Misterios es uno de los frutos más maduros del arte umbra de 1400 por su sentimiento religioso, su sencillez y su gracia: véanse los frescos de la Anunciación y de la Navidad. Aun más significativo, en el fresco de la Resurrección, es Alejandro VI arrodillado en el acto de rezar: es esto uno de los retratos históricos más

Pinturicchio: *Susanna and the Elders* - Pinturicchio: *Susana y los ancianos*
Pinturicchio: *Susanne et les vieillards* - Pinturicchio: *Susanna e i vecchioni*

maravillosos del Renacimiento, digno de ser comparado con el de Sixto IV por Melozzo de Forlí.

Sobre la puerta que pone en comunicación la Sala de los Santos con la de los Misterios se observa un fresco redondo, en que la Vírgen sostiene un libro abierto, mientras que el Niño, de pié sobre una almohada, parece absorto en la lectura; este fresco está reproducido en la portada de este volúmen.

En la Sala de los Santos, que reproduce acontecimientos sacados de la vida de los Santos, el arte de Pinturicchio debido a la vivacidad de la composición y al esplendor de los colores, alcanza a su perfección. Hay tan solo que observar a la dísputa de Santa Catalina, a la que arrímase la representación de la vuelta, por el agro romano, de una alegre compañía de cazadores. Sobre la parede al lado está pintada una escena de la vida de los hermitaños en el desierto, donde las tentaciones están representadas por un grupo de doncellas con alas de murciélago y cabelleras de donde asómanse los cuernos. Sigue el fresco de la Visitación, donde, un interior de casa, sobresale la representación de unas hiladoras que trabajan. También son dignos de nota los frescos de Santa Bárbara que huye perseguida por su padre y el de San Sebastián, donde, en el paesaje de fondo, el artista representó al Coliseo y a la Iglesia de los Santos Juán y Pablo. En la Sala de las Artes Liberales, que sigue la de los Santos, destácase el fresco de la Música, donde la Reina de todas las Armonías está rodeada por un coro de músicos que enseñan a sus instrumentos.

146

Pinturicchio: *St. Barbara Persecuted by her Father* - Pinturicchio: *Santa Bárbara perseguida por el padre*
Pinturicchio: *Sainte Barbe poursuivie par son père* - Pinturicchio: *S. Barbara perseguitata dal padre*

L'appartement des Borgia, au premier étage du palais de Nicolas V vers la grande cour du Belvédère, doit son nom et sa célébrité à Alexandre VI qui y ajouta la tour qui porte son nom et le fit décorer de fresques par l'ombrien Bernardino di Betto dit le Pinturicchio, lequel y travailla avec ses aides de 1492 à 1495. Il est composé de six salles dont la plus grande appelée Salle des Pontifes n'offre aucune trace du Pinturicchio. Le plafond de bois s'effondra en 1500 et fut rebâti en voûte sous Léon X qui le fit peindre par Pierin del Vaga et par Jean d'Udine. Aux quatre angles il y a de grands trophées aux armes des Médicis, et dans le tableau rond central on voit aussi des faunes dansants et des armoiries qui font allusion à la famille des Médicis. Dans les compartiments quadrangulaires qui renferment le tableau rond et dans les médaillons ovales peints au dessous figurent les principales planètes, les signes du Zodiaque et quelques constellation. Aux murs on peut voir et admirer six tapisseries d'art flamand du XVIe siècle reproduisant la légende de Céphale et Procris. D'autres tapisseries de proportions moindres, mais très fines, sont dans les autres salles: l'une d'elles représente le mariage de sainte Catherine, une autre le tableau de Raphaël dit le « Spasimo » de Sicile. Mais les salles principales, dans lesquelles resplendit l'art insurpassable du maître ombrien, ce sont les trois petites qui précèdent celle des Pontifes: la Salle des Mystères, la Salle des Saints et la Salle des Arts Libéraux.

La Salle des Mystères est un des fruits les plus mûrs de l'art ombrien du XVe siècle fait de sentiment religieux, de simplicité et de grâce. Encore plus significatif est, dans la fresque de la Résurrection, Alexandre VI qui prie à genoux. C'est un des merveilleux portraits historiques de la Renaissance, digne de prendre place à côté du Sixte IV de Melozzo da Forlí.

Pinturicchio: *The Annunciation* - Pinturicchio: *Anunciación*
Pinturicchio: *L'Annonciation* - Pinturicchio: *L'Annunciazione*

Au-dessus de la porte qui mène de la Salle des Saints à celle des Mystères on remarque un médaillon à fresque, dans lequel la Vierge Mère soutient un livre ouvert tandis que le Divin Enfant, dressé sur un coussin, semble en train de lire. Elle est reproduite au frontispice de ce volume.

Dans la Salle des Saints, qui reproduit des évènements tirés de la Vie des Saints, l'art du Pinturicchio, par la vivacité de la composition et la splendeur du coloris, touche la perfection. Il suffit d'observer la Dispute de sainte Catherine, qui a pour voisine une joyeuse compagnie de chasseurs revenant de la campagne romaine. Sur la paroi à droite il y a une fresque de la vie des anachorètes où les tentations sont raffigurées par un groupe de trois jeunes filles ayant des ailes de chauve-souris et la chevelure d'où pointent des cornes. Suit la fresque de la Visitation où dans un intérieur quelques fileuses au travail attirent e regard. D'autres fresques sont d'ailleurs dignes d'être notées: celle de sainte Barbe fuyant poursuivie par son père et celle de saint Sébastien où, dans le paysage du fond, l'artiste a représenté le Colisée et l'église des S. S. Giovanni et Paolo.

Dans la Salle des Arts Libéraux, qui fait suite à celle des Saints, il y a lieu de distinguer la fresque de la Musique, où la reine des harmonies trône entourée d'un chœur de musiciens qui font montre de leurs instruments.

Pinturicchio: *The Nativity* - Pinturicchio: *La Navidad*
Pinturicchio: *La Nativité* - Pinturicchio: *La Natività*

L'Appartamento Borgia, al primo piano del palazzo di Niccolò V verso il gran cortile di Belvedere, deve il suo nome e la sua celebrità ad Alessandro VI che vi aggiunse la torre che porta il suo nome e lo fece decorare di affreschi dall'umbro Bernardino di Betto, detto il Pinturicchio, il quale vi lavorò con i suoi aiuti dal 1492 al 1495. Consta di sei sale. La maggiore di esse è detta dei Pontefici, ma in essa non vi è traccia del Pinturicchio. Il soffitto di legno cadde nel 1500 e fu rifatto a volta sotto Leone X che lo fece dipingere da Pierin del Vaga e da Giovanni da Udine. Grandi trofei con le armi medicee sono nei quattro angoli; così pure nel tondo centrale si vedono fauni danzanti con insegne allusive alla famiglia dei Medici. Negli scomparti quadrangolari, che racchiudono il tondo centrale, e nei tondi ovali sottostanti sono raffigurati i pianeti maggiori, i segni dello zodiaco e alcune costellazioni. Appesi alle pareti si ammirano qui sei arazzi di arte fiamminga del '500 che riproducono la leggenda di Cefalo e Procri. Altri arazzi minori di proporzioni, ma finissimi, sono nelle altre sale: uno di essi rappresenta lo sposalizio di S. Caterina, un altro il quadro di Raffaello detto lo Spasimo di Sicilia. Ma le sale principali, in cui risplende in modo insuperabile l'arte del maestro umbro, sono le tre minori che precedono quella dei Pontefici: la sala dei Misteri, la sala dei Santi e la sala delle Arti Liberali.

La sala dei Misteri è uno dei frutti più maturi dell'arte umbra del '400 fatta di sentimento religioso, di semplicità e di grazia. Si vedano gli affreschi dell'Annunciazione e della Natività. Più significante ancora nell'affresco della Resurrezione è Alessandro VI inginocchiato in atto di preghiera. E' uno dei ritratti storici più meravigliosi del Rinascimento, degno di stare accanto a quello di Sisto IV di Melozzo da Forlì.

Pinturicchio: *The Dispute of St. Catherine* - Pinturicchio: *La dísputa de Santa Catalina*
Pinturicchio: *Dispute de sainte Catherine* - Pinturicchio: *La disputa di S. Caterina*

Sopra la porta che dalla sala dei Santi mette a quella dei Misteri si nota un tondo in affresco, nel quale la Vergine Madre sostiene un libro aperto, mentre il Divino Infante, ritto sopra un cuscino, sembra intento alla lettura. Esso è riprodotto nel frontespizio di questo volume.

Nella sala dei Santi, che riproduce avvenimenti tratti dalla vita dei Santi, l'arte del Pinturicchio, per la vivacità della composizione e lo splendore del colorito, tocca la perfezione. Basta osservare la disputa di S. Caterina, a cui si affianca il ritorno dalla campagna romana di un'allegra comitiva di caccia. Sulla parete accanto è dipinta una scena della vita degli anacoreti nel deserto, in cui le tentazioni sono raffigurate da un gruppo di tre donzelle con ali di pipistrello e dalla capigliatura dalla quale spuntano le corna. Segue l'affresco della Visitazione, dove, in un interno di casa, attirano lo sguardo alcune filatrici al lavoro. Sono pure degni di nota gli affreschi di S. Barbara che fugge inseguita dal padre e quello di S. Sebastiano, dove nel paesaggio di fondo l'artista ha rappresentato il Colosseo e la Chiesa dei SS. Giovanni e Paolo.

Nella sala delle Arti Liberali che fa seguito a quella dei Santi, va distinto l'affresco della Musica, in cui la regina delle armonie siede in trono circondata da un coro di musicanti che fanno mostra dei loro strumenti.

Pinturicchio: *The Dispute of St. Catherine* (detail)) - Pinturicchio: *La dísputa de Santa Catalina* (detalle)
Pinturicchio: *Dispute de sainte Catherine* (détail) - Pinturicchio: *La disputa di S. Caterina* (particolare)

151

Pinturicchio: *The Dispute of St. Catherine* (detail) - Pinturicchio: *La dísputa de Santa Catalina* (detalle)
Pinturicchio: *Dispute de sainte Catherine* (détail) - Pinturicchio: *La disputa di S. Caterina* (particolare)

152

Pinturicchio: *The Dispute of St. Catherine* (detail with two Horsemen)
Pinturicchio: *La dísputa de Santa Catalina* (detalle con dos caballeros)
Pinturicchio: *Dispute de sainte Catherine* (détail : deux chevaliers)
Pinturicchio: *La disputa di S. Caterina* (particolare con due cavalieri)

Pinturicchio: *Two Devils* - Pinturicchio: *Dos diablas*
Pinturicchio: *Deux diablesses* - Pinturicchio: *Due diavolesse*

154

Pinturicchio: *The Visitation* (detail with the Spinners) - Pinturicchio: *La Visitación* (detalle con las hiladoras)
Pinturicchio: *La Visitation* (détail: les fileuses) - Pinturicchio: *La Visitazione* (particolare con le filatrici)

Pinturicchio: *The Resurrection* (detail with Pope Alexander VI)
Pinturicchio: *La Resurrección* (detalle con el Papa Alejandro VI)
Pinturicchio: *La Résurrection* (détail: le pape Alexandre VI)
Pinturicchio: *La Resurrezione* (particolare col Papa Alessandro VI)

156

Tapestry of the Mystic Grapes (Hall of the Saints) - Tapiz del Racimo Místico (Sala de los Santos)
Tapisserie de la Grappe Mystique (Salle des Saints) - Arazzo del Grappolo Mistico (Sala dei Santi)

Tapestry of the Banquet (Hall of the Popes) - Tapiz del Banquete (Sala de los Pontífices)
Tapisserie du banquet (Salle des Pontifes) - Arazzo del banchetto (Sala dei Pontefici)

THE STANZE OF RAPHAEL

LAS CÁMARAS DE RAFAEL

LES STANZE DE RAPHAËL

LE STANZE DI RAFFAELLO

Raphael: *The Dispute of the Blessed Sacrament* (detail) - Rafael: *Disputa del SS. Sacramento* (detalle)
Raphaël: *Dispute du T. S. Sacrement* (détail) - Raffaello: *Disputa del SS. Sacramento* (particolare)

New marvels await the visitor in the Stanze of Raphael, where the apartment selected by Julius II used to be, and where also Leo X and his immediate successors lived. The Stanza della Segnatura is the oldest of them all and contains the oldest frescoes. Although of smaller dimensions, it compares worthily with the vault of the Sistine Chapel where, during the same years, Michelangelo was painting his poem of the Creation. The frescoes of the Segnatura represent the supreme elements in the spiritual development of mankind: Faith, which is conveyed through the mysteries of the Revelation and the acts of the Church; Knowledge, which is expressed by philosophy and the science of physics and mathematics; Justice, governed by the cardinal virtues and embodied in the civilian and ecclesiastical laws; the Fine Arts which with poetry and music, led by Apollo and the Muses, give joy and beauty to life.

After the Segnatura, and perhaps surpassing it in pictorial value, comes the Stanza of Heliodorus. Here historical events, full of movement, assume dramatic dress, while, from an artistic point of view, the subtle blending of color and shadows shows the influence of the greatest masters of the Venetian school.

The frescoes in the Stanze were begun toward the end of 1508, about fifteen years after those of Pinturicchio in the Borgia Apartment; but what a difference between the two works! Both excellent, no doubt, but so far apart in the artistic expression. In the halls of the Borgia Apartment we may see the limits reached by a pictorial art which derives, in form and spirit, from the miniature. In the Stanze, instead, we may admire an art which frees itself from the traditional schools, absorbing and surpassing them, and while revealing the influence of other masters, never loses its originality

Raphael: *The Burning of Borgo* - *Rafael*: Incendio de Borgo
Raphaël: *Incendie de Borgo* - Raffaello: *Incendio di Borgo*

or its balance until it passes into the hands of the pupils. Notice, for example, in the fresco of Heliodorus, the tranquil pace of the Papal retinue at the left, and the high priest absorbed in prayer in the center, in contrast with the terror, at the right, of the intruder fallen to the ground under the menacing fury of the angel on horseback. Notice also, in the Mass of Bolsena, the anguish of the priest celebrating mass in the midst of the bewildered faithful, on the left, and the calm expression of surprise of the Pope and his court, on the right. See finally, in the meeting of St. Leo the Great with Attila, the quiet advance of the Pope and the cardinals, as against the headlong rush of the invading barbarians. The frescoes of the Burning of Borgo were painted later and have less value, but even though they are not the direct work of the master they still reveal his vigilance in guiding and correcting his pupils.

Raphael: *The Dispute of the Blessed Sacrament* - Rafael: *Dísputa del SS. Sacramento*
Raphaël: *Dispute du T. S. Sacrement* - Raffaello: *Disputa del SS. Sacramento*

Nuevas maravillas esperan a los visitadores en las Cámaras de Rafael, donde estaba el aposento escojido por Julio II y donde León X y sus inmediatos sucesores tenían su habitación. La primera de las Cámaras, en el órden de tiempo y de los frescos, es la de la Signatura; aún sus dimensiones sean más reducidas, por su contenido ideal esta cámara puede compararse dignamente con la bóveda de la Capilla Sixtina, donde, en el mismo período, Miguel Ángel pintaba el poema de la Creación.

Los frescos de la Signatura representan el curso ideal de la humanidad en sus factores supremos: la Fe que se traduz en los misterios de la Revelación y en la acción de la Iglesia regida por la Teología; la Ciencia, de que son expresiones la filosofía y las doctrinas físicas y matemáticas; la Jurisprudencia, gobernada por las virtudes cardinales, que se concretiza en el derecho civil y eclesiástico y en los códigos relativos; y las Bellas Artes que, con la poesía y la música guiadas por Apolo, confortan y alegran la vida.

Luego después de la Signatura, sobrepasándola talvez como valor de pintura, viene la Cámara dicha del Heliodoro, donde los grandes acontecimientos de la historia, llenos de movimiento, asumen un aspecto dramático mientras que, bajo el punto de vista artístico, expertos matices de sombras y de colores indican la influencia de los mayores maestros de la escuela véneta.

Raphael: *Mt. Parnassus* - Rafael: *El Parnaso*
Raphaël: *Le Parnasse* - Raffaello: *Il Parnaso*

Los frescos de las Cámaras fueron empezados a fines de 1508, cerca de quince años
más tarde de los de Pinturicchio en el Aposento Borja: pero ¡ que diferencia entre las
dos obras ! Las dos excelentísimas, pero ¡ tan remotas como expresion artística ! En las
salas del Aposento vése el limite extremo a que podía llegar una pintura que, en su
espíritu y en sus formas, derivaba de la miniatura; en las Cámaras, a lo contrario,
admírase una pintura que se libra del vínculo de las escuelas tradicionales, absorbién-
dolas y sobrepasándolas a todas, con un movimiento ascendente que revela la influencia
de otros maestros pero no pierde a su originalidad y a su fuerza de equilibrio sino
cuando pasa en las manos de los discípulos. Véase justamente en el fresco del Heliodoro,
a la izquierda, la marcha sosegada de la procesión pontificia, el recogimiento del sumo
sacerdote al centro, contra el temor, a la derecha, del intruso bajo el furor amenazador
del ángel a caballo. Así en la Misa de Bolsena la agitación angustiosa del sacerdote
celebrante en medio del aturdimiento de los fieles a la izquiedra, y la compuesta mara-
villa del Papa y de su corte a la derecha; así, en el encuentro de San León Magno
con Átila, el tranquillo adelantarse del Papa y de los Cardenales y el precipitarse hacia
adelante de los bárbaros invasores.
Sea como valor que en órden de tiempo, siguen los frescos del Incendio de Borgo; tambien en estos, aún falte la obra directa del maestro, obsérvase siempre su acción vigilante en corregir y guiar la mano de sus discípulos.

164

Raphael: *Propertius and Petrarch* (detail of « Mt. Parnassus ») - Rafael: *Propercio y Petrarca* (detalle del « Parnaso »)
Raphaël: *Properce et Pétrarque* (détail du « Parnasse ») - Raffaello: *Properzio e Petrarca* (particolare del « Parnaso »)

D'autres merveilles attendent le visiteur dans les salles de Raphaël où fut l'appartement préféré de Jules II et où habitèrent Léon X et ses successeurs immédiats. La première des « stanze » dans la succession du temps et des fresques est celle de la Signature. Quoique de petites dimensions, cette salle par son contenu idéal est digne d'être comparée à la voûte de la Sixtine, où à la même époque Michel-Ange peignait le poème de la Création.

Les fresques de la Signature représentent le cours spirituel de l'humanité: la Foi qui se traduit dans les mystères de la Révélation et dans l'action de la Théologie; la Science dont la philosophie et les sciences physiques et mathématiques sont l'expression; la Jurisprudence gouvernée par les vertus cardinales et qui se précise dans le droit civil et le droit ecclésiastique et dans leurs codes respectifs; les Beaux-Arts qui, avec la poésie et la musique précédées par Apollon et par les Muses, consolent et réjouissent la Vie. A côté de la Signature, et la surpassant peut-être, vient la Salle dite d'Héliodore où les grands événements de l'histoire, remplis d'agitation, prennent une forme dramatique, tandis que, du point de vue artistique, les savantes nuances d'ombres et de couleurs accusent l'influence des grands maîtres de l'école vénitienne.

Les fresques des Salles prirent naissance à la fin de 1508, environ quinze ans après celles du Pinturicchio dans l'Appartement des Borgia, mais quelle différence entre les deux œuvres ! L'une et l'autre excellentes, mais si éloignées quant à l'expression arti-

Raphael: *The School of Athens* - Rafael: *La Escuela de Aténas*
Raphaël: *L'École d'Athènes* - Raffaello: *La Scuola d'Atene*

stique. C'est dans les salles de l'Appartement des Borgia qu'on voit l'extrême limite
à laquelle pouvait aboutir un art de peindre qui par son esprit et ses formes dérivait
de la miniature; dans les « Stanze » on découvre une peinture qui se libère des écoles
traditionnelles mais les absorbe toutes et les surpasse par un mouvement ascendant
qui révèle l'influence d'autres maîtres, sans perdre son originalité ni sa force d'équilibre,
sauf quand elle passe aux mains des élèves.

Il suffit de voir, en effet, dans la fresque d'Héliodore, la marche tranquille du cortège
pontifical sur la gauche, le recueillement du grand'prêtre en prière au centre, contre
l'effarement, à droite, de l'intrus tombé à terre sous la menaçante irruption de l'ange
à cheval. De même aussi dans la Messe de Bolsena le trouble angoissé du prêtre cé-
lébrant parmi la stupéfaction des fidèles à gauche, et l'étonnement réservé du Pape
et de sa cour à droite; de même dans la rencontre de saint Léon-le-Grand avec Attila,
le mouvement paisible du Pape qui se porte en avant avec ses cardinaux, et la ruée
des barbares envahisseurs. Viennent après, pour ce qui est du temps et de la valeur,
les fresques de l'Incendie de Borgo, mais où, à défaut de l'exécution directe du maître,
son action vigilante n'a pas laissé de guider et de corriger celle des élèves.

166

Raphael: *The Mass of Bolsena* - Rafael: *La Misa de Bolsena*
Raphaël: *La Messe de Bolsena* - Raffaello: *La Messa di Bolsena*

Nuove meraviglie attendono il visitatore nelle Stanze di Raffaello, dove fu l'appartamento prescelto da Giulio II, e dove abitarono Leone X ed i suoi immediati successori. La prima delle Stanze, nella successione del tempo e degli affreschi, è quella della Segnatura. Benchè di dimensioni minori, per il suo contenuto ideale questa stanza si confronta degnamente con la volta della Sistina, dove, negli anni medesimi, Michelangelo dipingeva il poema della Creazione.

Gli affreschi della Segnatura rappresentano il corso ideale dell'umanità nei suoi fattori supremi: la Fede che si traduce nei misteri della Rivelazione e nell'azione della Chiesa retta dalla Teologia; la Scienza di cui sono espressione la filosofia e le dottrine fisiche e matematiche; la Giurisprudenza governata dalle virtù cardinali e che si concreta nel diritto civile ed ecclesiastico e nei codici relativi; le Belle Arti che con la poesia e la musica guidata da Apollo e dalle Muse confortano e rallegrano la vita.

Viene accanto alla Segnatura, e per valore pittorico forse la supera, la Stanza detta dell'Eliodoro, dove i grandi avvenimenti della storia, pieni di movimento, assumono veste drammatica, mentre, nei riguardi artistici, sapienti sfumature di ombre e di colori accennano all'influsso dei maggiori maestri della scuola veneta.

Gli affreschi delle Stanze ebbero inizio alla fine del 1508, circa quindici anni dopo quelli del Pinturicchio nell'Appartamento Borgia; ma quale differenza tra le due opere!

Raphael: *The Expulsion of Heliodorus from the Temple* - Rafael: *La Cazada de Heliodoro del Templo*
Raphaël: *Héliodore chassé du temple* - Raffaello: *La cacciata di Eliodoro dal Tempio*

Eccellentissime entrambe, ma ben lontane fra loro nell'espressione artistica. Nelle sale dell'Appartamento Borgia si vede l'estremo limite a cui poteva giungere un'arte pittorica che nello spirito e nelle forme derivava dalla miniatura; nelle Stanze si scorge una pittura che si svincola dalle scuole tradizionali, ma tutte le assorbe e la supera, con un movimento ascendente che rivela l'influsso di altri maestri, ma non perde la sua originalità e la sua forza d'equilibrio, se non quando passa nelle mani degli scolari. Vedasi appunto, nell'affresco dell'Eliodoro, il tranquillo incedere a sinistra del corteo pontificio, il raccoglimento del sommo sacerdote in preghiera al centro, contro lo sgomento, a destra, dell'intruso caduto a terra sotto la furia minacciosa dell'angelo a cavallo. Così nella Messa di Bolsena il turbamento angoscioso del sacerdote celebrante in mezzo allo sbalordimento dei fedeli a sinistra, e la composta meraviglia del Papa e della sua corte a destra; così, nell'incontro di S. Leone Magno con Attila, il tranquillo avanzarsi del Papa e dei cardinali e il precipitarsi in avanti dei barbari invasori.

Vengono dopo per tempo e per valore gli affreschi dell'Incendio di Borgo, ma dove, pur mancando l'opera diretta del maestro, si manifesta sempre l'azione vigile di lui nel guidare e correggere quella degli scolari.

168

Raphael: *The Dispute of the Blessed Sacrament* (detail) - Rafael: *Dísputa del SS. Sacramento* (detalle)
Raphaël: *Dispute du T. S. Sacrement* (détail) - Raffaello: *Disputa del SS. Sacramento* (particolare)

**169**

Raphael: *The Dispute of the Blessed Sacrament* (detail) - Rafael: *Disputa del SS. Sacramento* (detalle)
Raphaël: *Dispute du T. S. Sacrement* (détail) - Raffaello: *Disputa del SS. Sacramento* (particolare)

Raphael: *The Dispute of the Blessed Sacrament* (detail) - Rafael: *Dísputa del SS. Sacramento* (detalle)
Raphaël: *Dispute du T. S. Sacrement* (détail) - Raffaello: *Disputa del SS. Sacramento* (particolare)

Raphael: *The Dispute of the Blessed Sacrament* (detail) - Rafael: *Dísputa del SS. Sacramento* (detalle)
Raphaël: *Dispute du T. S. Sacrament* (détail) - Raffaello: *Disputa del SS. Sacramento* (particolare)

Raphael: *The Dispute of the Blessed Sacrament* (detail) - Rafael: *Dísputa del SS. Sacramento* (detalle)
Raphaël: *Dispute du T. S. Sacrement* (détail) - Raffaello: *Disputa del SS. Sacramento* (particolare)

Raphael: *The Dispute of the Blessed Sacrament* (detail) - Rafael: *Dísputa del SS. Sacramento* (detalle)
Raphaël: *Dispute du T. S. Sacrement* (détail) - Raffaello: *Disputa del SS. Sacramento* (particolare)

Raphael: *The Dispute of the Blessed Sacrament* (detail) - Rafael: *Dísputa del SS. Sacramento* (detalle)
Raphaël: *Dispute du T. S. Sacrement* (détail) - Raffaello: *Disputa del SS. Sacramento* (particolare)

173

Raphael: *Apollo and Marsyas* - Rafael: *Apolo e Marsia*
Raphaël: *Apollon et Marsyas* - Raffaello: *Apollo e Marsia*

Raphael: *Mt. Parnassus* (detail with two Muses) - Rafael: *El Parnaso* (detalle con dos Musas)
Raphaël: *Le Parnasse* (détail de deux Muses) - Raffaello: *Il Parnaso* (particolare con due Muse)

Raphael: *The School of Athens* (Heraclitus) - Rafael: *La Escuela de Aténas* (Heráclito)
Raphaël: *L'École d'Athènes* (Héraclite) - Raffaello: *La Scuola d'Atene* (Eraclito)

Raphael: *The School of Athens* (Head of Aristotle) - Rafael: *La Escuela de Aténas* (Cabeza de Aristóteles)
Raphaël: *L'École d'Athènes* (Tête d'Aristote) - Raffaello: *La Scuola d'Atene* (Testa di Aristotele)

Raphael: *The Mass of Bolsena* (detail) - Rafael: *La Misa de Bolsena* (detalle)
Raphaël: *La Messe de Bolsena* (détail) - Raffaello: *La Messa di Bolsena* (particolare)

Raphael: *The Mass of Bolsena* (detail with Chair-bearers) - Rafael: *La Misa de Bolsena* (detalle con los sillarios)
Raphaël: *La Messe de Bolsena* (détail) - Raffaello: *La Messa di Bolsena* (particolare coi sediarii)

Raphael: *The Mass of Bolsena* (detail) - Rafael: *La Misa de Bolsena* (detalle)
Raphaël: *La Messe de Bolsena* (détail) - *Raffaello: La Messa di Bolsena* (particolare)

Raphael: *The Liberation of St. Peter from Prison* (detail) - Rafael: *Liberación de San Pedro del cárcel* (detalle)
Raphaël: *Saint Pierre libéré du cachot* (détail) - Raffaello: *Liberazione di S. Pietro dal carcere* (particolare)

181

Raphael: *St. Leo Stopping Attila* (detail) - Rafael: *San León que para a Átila* (detalle)
Raphaël: *Saint Léon arrêtant Attila* (détail) - Raffaello: *S. Leone che ferma Attila* (particolare)

182

THE  LOGGIA  OF  RAPHAEL

LA  LOGIA  DE  RAFAEL

LA  LOGE  DE  RAPHAËL

LA  LOGGIA  DI  RAFFAELLO

Loggia of Raphael: View of the whole - Logia de Rafael: Vista de conjunto
Loge de Raphaël: Vue générale - Loggia di Raffaello: Veduta d'assieme

The Building of the Ark - Construcción del Arca
Construction de l'Arche - Costruzione dell'Arca

The Loggia of Raphael may be considered a splendid complement to the Stanze.
It is inspired by the « grotesque », a name designating the paintings and reliefs which
were then being discovered among the ruins of the ancient imperial dwellings of the
Palatine and the Esquiline. Raphael, who succeeded Bramante in the work of fin-
ishing the Belvedere Loggias ordered by Julius II, conceived and directed its decoration.
The plan and a great part of the designs are certainly his own work; those who executed his ideas were the pupils who had already collaborated with him in the last
Stanze: principally Giovanni Penni, Giulio Romano, Perin del Vaga and Giovanni
da Udine.
The Loggia extends the length of thirteen arcades: the walls, pillars and underparts
of the arches are covered with arabesques and moldings which reveal the inexhaust-
ible fantasy and most refined taste of the artists. The frescoes of the vaults, four
for each arcade, represent the principal episodes of the Old Testament, from the creation of the world to the building of the Temple of Solomon. Only the thirteenth arcade contains scenes from the New Testament. If Raphael did not actually work here
with his brush, his genius is evident everywhere as inspirer and guide; and despite
the irreparable damages of time, it awakens in the observer the most fervent admiration.

186

Moses Rescued from the Waters - Moisés salvado de las aguas
Moïse sauvé des eaux - Mosè salvato dalle acque

Como un espléndido aditamento a las Cámaras debe ser considerada la Logia de Rafael, que saca su inspiración de las « grutescas », nombre con que ses designaron las pinturas y los frescos que ian descubriéndose entonces entre las antiguas moradas de los Emperadores encima del Esquilino y del Palatino.

Rafael, que había sucedido a Bramante en el encargo de completar a las logias de Belvedere, ideadas por Julio II, proyectó y dirigió a la decoración. Obras suyas son sin duda el proyecto y la mayoría de los dibujos; la ejecución fué confiada a los discípulos que ya habían colaborado con el en las últimas Cámaras, y especialmente Giovanni Penni, Giulio Romano, Perin del Vaga y Giovanni de Udine.

La Logia extiéndese por trece arcos. Las paredes, los pilares y los intradoses están cubiertos de arabescos y de estucos que indican en los artístas una fantasía excepcional y el gosto más refinado. Los frescos de las bóvedas, cuatro por cada arco, representan episodios del Antiguo Testamento, desde la creación del mundo hasta la erección del Templo de Salomón. Tan solo el último arco contiene escenas del Nuevo Testamento. Aún Rafael no tenga obrado aquí materialmente con su pincel, su genio está presente doquiera como inspirador y guía y, a pesar de los daños gravísimos del tiempo, despierta en el observador la admiración la más viva.

Jacob's Dream - El sueño de Jacob
Le songe de Jacob - Il sogno di Giacobbe

La « Loggia » de Raphaël est considérée comme un splendide appendice des « Stanze ». Elle tire son inspiration des « grotesques », nom sous lequel on désignait les peintures et les stucs que l'on découvrait alors parmi les ruines des maisons antiques du Palatin et de l'Esquilin. Raphaël, qui avait succédé à Bramante pour l'achèvement des loges du Belvédère commandées par Jules II, en conçut et dirigea l'exécution. Le projet et les dessins pour une bonne part sont certainement son œuvre; les exécuteurs en furent les disciples qui avaient déjà collaboré avec lui dans les dernières « Stanze »: notamment Giovanni Penni, Jules Romain, Perin del Vaga et Jean d'Udine.

La loge dans son étendue forme treize arcades; les parois, les piliers et les arcs-doubleaux sont couverts d'arabesques et de stucs qui prouvent chez les artistes une fantaisie intarissable et le goût le plus raffiné. Les fresques des voûtes, quatre pour chaque arcade, représentent les épisodes principaux de l'Ancien Testament, depuis la création du monde jusqu'à l'érection du Temple de Salomon. La treizième arcade seule contient des scènes du Nouveau Testament. Si Raphaël n'a pas ici travaillé matériellement de son pinceau, son génie n'en est pas moins partout présent comme inspirateur et guide, et malgré les outrages irréparables du temps éveille chez l'observateur la plus vive admiration.

188

Rebecca and Abimelech - Rebeca y Abimeleck
Rébecca et Abimelech - Rebecca ed Abimelech

Come splendida appendice alle Stanze va considerata la Loggia di Raffaello. Essa trae
la sua ispirazione dalle « grottesche », nome col quale furono designati i dipinti e gli
stucchi che si scoprivano allora tra le rovine delle antiche dimore imperiali del Palatino
e dell'Esquilino.

Raffaello che era successo a Bramante nell'incarico di condurre a termine le logge di
Belvedere, ordinate da Giulio II, ne ideò e diresse la decorazione. Opera sua sono certa-
mente il progetto e gran parte dei disegni: ne furono esecutori i discepoli che già avevano
collaborato con lui nelle ultime Stanze: principalmente Giovanni Penni, Giulio Romano,
Perin del Vaga e Giovanni da Udine.

La Loggia si estende per tredici arcate; le pareti, i pilastri e i sottarchi sono coperti
di arabeschi e di stucchi che dimostrano negli artisti una fantasia inesauribile e il gusto
più raffinato. Gli affreschi delle volte, quattro per ogni arcata, rappresentano i principali episodi dell'Antico Testamento, dalla creazione del mondo all'erezione del tempio
di Salomone. Soltanto la tredicesima arcata contiene scene del Nuovo Testamento. Se
l'Urbinate non ha operato materialmente qui col suo pennello, il suo genio è presente
dappertutto come ispiratore e guida, e, nonostante i danni irreparabili del tempo, desta
nell'osservatore la più viva ammirazione.

Joseph and Potiphar's Wife - José y la Mujer de Putifar
Joseph et la femme de Putiphar - Giuseppe e la moglie di Putifarre

Joseph Interprets his Dreams to his Brothers - José explica los sueños a sus hermanos
Joseph explique leurs songes à ses frères - Giuseppe spiega i sogni ai suoi fratelli

THE TAPESTRY GALLERY

LA GALERÍA DE LOS TAPICES

LA GALERIE DES TAPISSERIES

LA GALLERIA DEGLI ARAZZI

The Nativity - La Navidad - Noël - Il Natale

From the beginning of the Renaissance tapestries were, together with paintings, one of the favorite ornaments of the Papal apartments. The most famous ones, commissioned by Leo X to decorate the Sistine Chapel, were to represent the principal events in the life of Christ and of the Apostles. Raphael, assisted by his disciples, designed and painted the first ten cartoons which were sent to the workshop of Peter Van Aelst in Brussels to be woven. Seven of them were in their places in the Sistine Chapel in time for St. Stephen's day in 1519, and the other three arrived in later years. These tapestries were called « of the old school » to distinguish them from those, also woven in Brussels, which were designed by Raphael's pupils, probably after some sketch of the master, and which were sent to Rome only in 1530, when Clement VII was Pope: these were called tapestries « of the new school ». The tapestries of the old school are kept in the Pinacoteca, in the great Hall of Raphael (see, in particular, those of the Miraculous Draught of Fishes and the Consignment of the Keys, pages 194, 196). The tapestries of the new school are exhibited, with some others of various workshops, in the Tapestry Gallery, which leads from the Gallery of the Candelabra to the Map Gallery. Especially admirable for their feeling and their coloring are those representing the Nativity and the Resurrection (pages 193, 195).

193

14

The Miraculous Draught of Fishes - La pesca milagrosa - La Pêche miraculeuse - La pesca miracolosa

Desde hace los primeros años del Renacimiento, los tapices eran, junto con las pinturas, uno de los adornos preferidos de los aposentos pontificios. Los tapices más afamados, encargados por Leon X para decorar a la Capilla Sixtina, debían representar los acontecimientos principales de la vida de Jesucristo y de los Apóstoles. Rafael, con la ayuda de sus discípulos, dibujó y pintó a los primeros diez cartones que fueron enviados para tejer al taller de Pietro van Aelst de Bruselas. Por la fiesta de San Esteban de 1519 siete de ellos ya estaban en su lugar en la Capilla Sixtina, mientras que los demás llegaron en los años sucesivos. Estos fueron dichos « de la vieja escuela » para distinguirlos de aquellos, también tejidos en Bruselas, que fueron dibujados por los discípulos de Rafael, probablemente con el ayuda de esbozos originales del Maestro, que fueron despachados a Roma tán solo en 1530 bajo el pontificado de Clemente VII; esto fueron llmados « tapices de nueva escuela ».

Los tapices de la vieja escuela están custodiados en la Pinacoteca, en la gran sala de Rafael (véanse, por ejemplo, los de la Pesca milagrosa y de la Entrega de las llaves (págs. 194, 196). Los de la nueva escuela están expuestos, junto con unos otros de fábricas diferentes, en la Galería homónima, que sirve como pasaje desde la Galería de los Candelabros a la de los Mapas Geográficos. Admirables por sentimiento y colores son tambíen los que representan la Navidad y la Resurrección (págs. 193, 195).

The Resurrection - La Resurrección - La Résurrection - La Resurrezione

Jusqu'aux premières années de la Renaissance les tapisseries étaient avec les peintures un des ornements préférés des appartements pontificaux. Les plus célèbres d'entre elles, commandées par Léon X pour décorer la Chapelle Sixtine, devaient représenter les faits principaux de la Vie de Jésus et des Apôtres. Raphaël, aidé de ses élèves, dessina et peignit les dix premiers cartons qui furent envoyés pour le tissage à l'atelier de Pierre van Aelst de Bruxelles. Pour la fête de saint Etienne en 1519, sept d'entre elles occupaient leur poste à la Chapelle Sixtine et les trois autres arrivèrent au cours des années suivantes. Elle furent dites de la *vieille école* pour les distinguer d'autres, tissues également à Bruxelles, et dessinées par les élèves de Raphaël qui selon toute vraisemblance avaient profité de quelques ébauches du maître. Celles-ci furent expédiées à Rome en 1530 seulement sous le pontificat de Clément VIII, d'où leur nom de tapisseries de la *nouvelle école*.

Les tapisseries de la *vieille école* sont gardées dans la Pinacothèque, dans la Salle de Raphaël, où elles font une escorte d'honneur au maître (voir, par exemple, celles de la Pêche miraculeuse et de la Remise des clefs (pages 194, 196). Celles de la *nouvelle école* sont exposées avec quelques autres de différents ateliers dans la Galerie ainsi appelée qui sert de passage de la Galerie des Candélabres à celle des Cartes Géographiques. Un sentiment admirable, et aussi leurs coloris, distinguent celles qui représentent la Nativité et la Résurrection (pages 193, 195).

The Consignment of the Keys - La entrega de las llaves - La Remise des clefs - La consegna delle chiavi

Fino dai primi anni del Rinascimento, insieme coi dipinti, gli arazzi erano uno degli ornamenti preferiti degli appartamenti pontifici. I più celebri di essi, ordinati da Leone X per decorare la Cappella Sistina, dovevano rappresentare i fatti principali della vita di Gesù e degli Apostoli. Raffaello, coadiuvato dai suoi scolari, disegnò e dipinse i primi dieci cartoni che furono mandati per la tessitura all'officina di Pietro Van Aelst di Bruxelles. Per la festa di S. Stefano del 1519 sette di essi erano al loro posto nella Cappella Sistina, e gli altri tre arrivarono negli anni successivi. Furono detti della *vecchia scuola* per distinguerli da quelli tessuti pure a Bruxelles, che furono disegnati dagli scolari di Raffaello, i quali si valsero verosimilmente di qualche abbozzo del maestro e che furono spediti a Roma soltanto nel 1530, sotto il pontificato di Clemente VII; di qui il loro nome di arazzi della *nuova scuola*.

Gli arazzi della *vecchia scuola* sono custoditi nella Pinacoteca, nella grande sala di Raffaello, in cui fanno scorta d'onore al maestro (vedi, per esempio, quelli della Pesca miracolosa e della Consegna delle chiavi, pagg. 194, 196). Quelli della *nuova scuola* sono esposti con pochi altri di diverse fabbriche nella Galleria omonima, che serve di passaggio dalla Galleria dei Candelabri a quella delle Carte Geografiche. Mirabili per sentimento ed anche per colorito sono quelli che rappresentano la Natività e la Risurrezione (pagg. 193, 195).

196

THE MAP GALLERY

LA GALERÍA DE LOS MAPAS GEOGRÁFICOS

LA GALERIE DES CARTES GÉOGRAPHIQUES

LA GALLERIA DELLE CARTE GEOGRAFICHE

View of the Map Gallery - Vista de la Galería de los Mapas Geográficos
Vue de la Galerie des Cartes Géographiques - Veduta della Galleria delle Carte Geografiche

This Gallery is an eloquent document of the interest in geography that was aroused by the great discoveries at the end of the fifteenth century and the first decades of the sixteenth. Stories and descriptions of the voyages were diffused by the printing press; navigation maps became popular and were used as an object of decoration for mural frescoes in castles and palaces.

Gregory XIII, not content with having erected as an observation post the Tower of the Winds in the West Wing of the Belvedere Court, decided to have also, in the interior of the Palace, a convenient space for reproducing maps. With this in mind, he invited from Florence the Dominican Father Ignazio Danti, one of the great mathematicians and cosmographers of his time, and had him draw the maps of the world, as it was then known, on the walls of the third Loggia. On the third floor along the West side of the Belvedere Court, in a gallery 390 feet long, he had the walls decorated with reproductions of the states and regions of Italy, from the Alps to Malta and from Corsica to Istria and Dalmatia. Here we can distinguish the ports of Genoa, Venice, Ancona, Malta, etc., and on the sea fantastic monsters and all kinds of commercial ships and pleasure boats.

The vaults are divided by beautiful plaster moldings in geometric sections which are covered by inscriptions and numerous frescoes. In these paintings some very skillful artists of the sixteenth century and the first half of the seventeenth represented persons and events related to the regions described on the walls beneath.

Christopher Columbus on the Ligurian Sea - Cristobal Colón en el mar de Liguria
Christophe Colomb dans la mer de Ligurie - Cristoforo Colombo nel mare di Liguria

Esta Galería es un documento elocuente del fervor para con los estudios geográficos despertado por las grandes descubiertas de los navegadores a fines del siglo XV y en los primeros decenios del siglo XVI, a raíz de las cuales difundiéronse por la imprenta narraciones y descripciones de viajes, multiplicáronse los mapas de navegación y introdújose la costumbre de emplear mapas como objetos de decoración para frescos murales en los castillos y en los palacios públicos y particulares.

Además de mandar edificar, en el ala de poniente del patio de Belvedere, la Torre de los Vientos que había de servir para observaciones astronómicas, Gregorio XIII quizo que también en el interior del Palacio se destinara un espacio adecuado para la reproducción de mapas geográficos. Para este fin convidó él de Florencia a Roma el Padre dominicano Ignacio Danti, uno de los primeros matemáticos y cosmógrafos de sus tiempos, y le hizo dibujar sobre las paredes de la tercera Logia los mapas del globo conocidos entonces; también destinó una galería de 120 metros de largo al tercero piso del lado occidental del patio de Belvedere, para que allí fueran reproducidos los Estados y las Regiones de Italia desde los Alpes a Malta y desde la Córcega a la Istria y a la Dalmacia. Destácanse los puertos de Génova, de Venecia, de Ancona, de Malta, etc. y las aguas del mar están esparcidas de monstruos fantásticos y de naves de transporte y de deporte de formas diferentes.

Las bóvedas están divididas por hermosas cornisas de estuco en reparticiones geométricas con inscripciones y muchísimos frescos donde, rivalizando entre si, expertos pintores entre fines de 1500 y la primera mitad de 1600 representaron personajes y acontecimientos característicos de las regiones descritas en las paredes abajo.

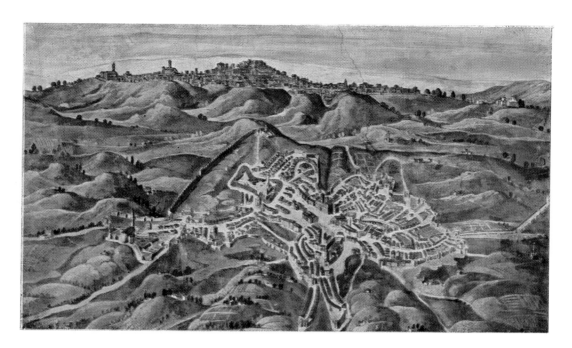

Plan and Prospect of Perugia - Plantilla y perfil de Perugia
Plan et profil de Pérouse - Pianta e profilo di Perugia

Cette Galerie est un document éloquent de la ferveur pour les études géographiques suscitées par les grandes découvertes des navigateurs sur la fin du XV<sup>e</sup> siècle et durant la première partie du XVI<sup>e</sup>. C'est grâce à ces découvertes que se répandirent, par le moyen de l'imprimerie, les narrations et les descriptions de voyages, que les cartes de navigation se multiplièrent, et que s'introduisit la coutume d'en faire des objets de décoration pour fresques murales dans les châteaux et dans les palais publics et privés. Non content d'avoir érigé pour les observations, dans l'aile ouest de la cour du Belvédère, la Tour des Vents, Grégoire XIII voulut aussi que des locaux satisfaisants fussent aménagés pour la reproduction des cartes géographiques. A cette fin il invita à venir de Florence à Rome le P. dominicain Ignazio Danti, un des premiers mathématiciens et cosmographes de son temps, et fit dessiner par lui sur les murs de la troisième Loge les cartes du globe alors connues, et voulut que dans une Galerie longue de 120 m., au troisième étage du côté occidental de la cour du Belvédère, fussent reproduits les Etats et les régions de l'Italie depuis la ligne des Alpes jusqu'à Malte et de la Corse à l'Istrie et à la Dalmatie. On y distingue les ports de Gênes, de Venise, d'Ancône, de Malte, etc., et sur les eaux de la mer sont disséminés des monstres imaginaires et maintes formes de nefs de transport et de plaisir.

Les voûtes sont divisées par de légers cadres de stuc en compartiments géométriques dans lesquels se lisent des inscriptions et sont insérées de nombreuses fresques où rivalisent d'excellents peintres qui, durant la fin du XVI<sup>e</sup> siècle et la première moitié du XVII<sup>e</sup>, ont figuré des personnages et des événements particuliers aux régions décrites sur les murs au-dessous.

201

Port of Ancona (detail) - El puerto de Ancona (detalle)
Le port d'Ancône (détail) - Il porto di Ancona (particolare)

Questa Galleria è un documento eloquente del fervore per gli studi geografici susci-
tati dalle grandi scoperte dei navigatori sulla fine del sec. XV e nei primi decenni del
sec. XVI, e per le quali si diffusero per la stampa narrazioni e descrizioni di viaggi,
si moltiplicarono le carte di navigazione e s'introdusse l'uso di farne oggetto di decorazione per affreschi murali nei castelli e nei palazzi pubblici e privati.

Gregorio XIII, non contento di aver eretto per le osservazioni, nell'ala di ponente del
cortile di Belvedere, la Torre dei Venti, volle che anche nell'interno del Palazzo fosse
dato uno spazio conveniente alla riproduzione delle carte geografiche. A questo scopo
egli invitò da Firenze a Roma il P. domenicano Ignazio Danti, uno dei primi mate-
matici e cosmografi del suo tempo, e da lui fece disegnare sulle pareti della terza Loggia
le carte del globo allora conosciute, e volle che in una galleria lunga m. 120, al terzo
piano del fianco occidentale del cortile di Belvedere, fossero riprodotti gli Stati e le
regioni dell'Italia dalla cerchia delle Alpi a Malta e dalla Corsica all'Istria e alla Dal-
mazia. Vi si distinguono i porti di Genova, di Venezia, di Ancona, di Malta, ecc., e
sulle acque del mare sono disseminati mostri fantastici e diverse foggie di navi da
trasporto e da diporto.

Le volte sono divise con leggiadre cornici di stucco, in reparti geometrici in cui si leg-
gono iscrizioni e s'inquadrano moltissimi affreschi, dove, gareggiando tra loro, valenti
pittori, tra la fine del 1500 e la prima metà del '600, rappresentarono personaggi ed
avvenimenti propri delle regioni descritte nelle pareti sottostanti.

202

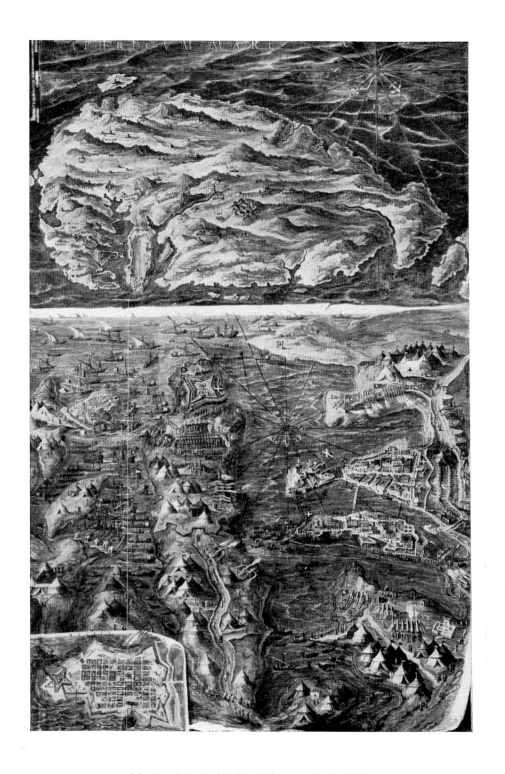

Island and Port of Malta - Isla y puerto de Malta
Ile et port de Malte - Isola e porto di Malta

Port of Genoa - Puerto de Génova - Le port de Gênes - Il porto di Genova

Port of Venice - Puerto de Venecia - Le port de Venise - Il porto di Venezia

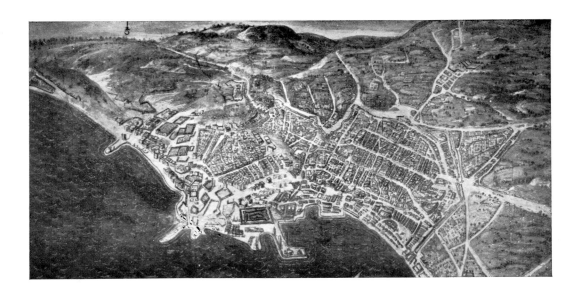

View of Naples - Vista de Nápoles - Vue de Naples - Veduta di Napoli

View of Syracuse - Vista de Siracusa - Vue de Syracuse - Veduta di Siracusa

206

View of Urbino - Vista de Urbino - Vue d'Urbin - Veduta di Urbino

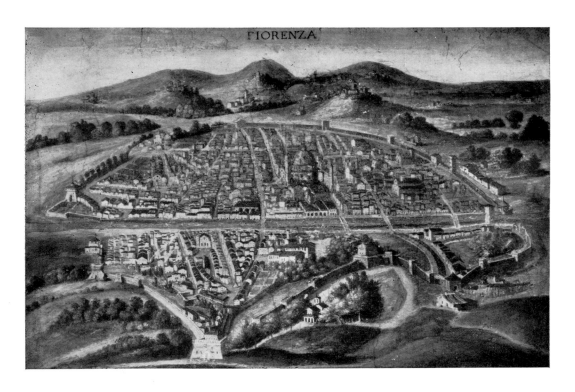

View of Florence - Vista de Florencia - Vue de Florence - Veduta di Firenze

Plan of Milan - Plantilla de Milán - Plan de Milan - Pianta di Milano

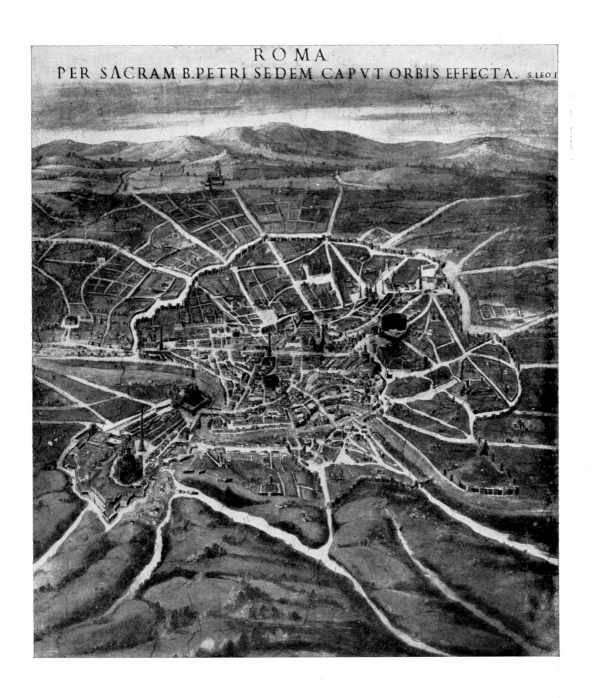

ROMA
PER SACRAM B. PETRI SEDEM CAPVT ORBIS EFFECTA. S. LEO. I

Plan of Rome - Plantilla de Roma - Plan de Rome - Pianta di Roma

15

View of the Tremiti Islands - Vista de las Islas Trémites
Vue des iles Tremiti - Veduta delle isole Tremiti

THE  VATICAN  LIBRARY

LA  BIBLIOTECA  VATICANA

LA  BIBLIOTHÈQUE  VATICANE

LA  BIBLIOTECA  VATICANA

Vatican Library: Great Hall of Sixtus V - Biblioteca Vaticana: Salón de Sixto V
Bibliothèque du Vatican: Salle de Sixte-Quint - Biblioteca Vaticana: Salone di Sisto V

The Vatican Library is the most important in the whole world, if not for the number of books, certainly for the value of its manuscripts which embrace every phase and aspect of civilization. The important contents of the Library are enhanced by the splendor of the surroundings, as its exhibition halls compare well, in beauty of ornamentation and in the interesting subjects of the paintings, with the Map Gallery already described. A typical example is the great Sistine Hall (about 240 ft. by 50) which, divided by pillars into two naves, occupies the top floor of the palace commissioned by Sixtus V across the Belvedere Court. This hall is covered from top to bottom with frescoes having for their theme the glorification of books and of the building enterprises which have immortalized the name of this energetic Pope.

On the great pillars we may admire the mythical figures of the inventors of the alphabet; on the side walls are represented the most celebrated Libraries of history and the Church Councils in which the truth contained in the books was defended. Above, in the lunettes, are represented the monumental works which were achieved by the same Pope in the brief space of five years: works which altered the face of Rome and gave it the general appearance it has today. Princely gifts and autographs of

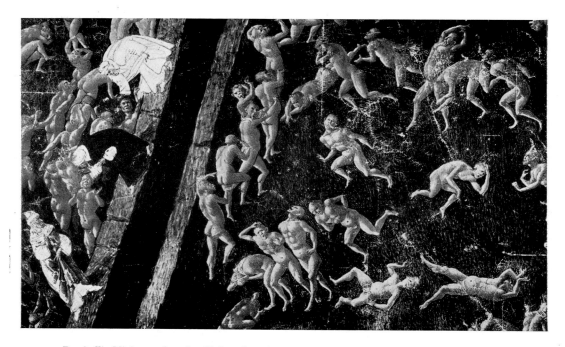

Botticelli: Miniature for the Divine Comedy - Botticelli: Miniatura para la Divina Comedia
Botticelli: Miniature pour la Divine Comédie - Botticelli: Miniatura per la Divina Commedia

especial importance are exhibited on the beautiful marble and bronze tables which are placed between the pillars. But the greatest treasures are in the show cases along the western nave, where we may admire the most valuable and rare documents, from the earliest manuscript of the Bible in the Greek version, known as the Septuagint, to the letter addressed in 1613 by the Japanese Prince Mutsu to Paul V.

Here are reproduced as samples some miniatures from the Vatican manuscript of Virgil, and from the Joshua Roll: these show the last phase of the classic art of the fourth and fifth centuries after Christ and anticipate the byzantine art of the seventh and eighth centuries. Very significant is Botticelli's illumination of Dante's Inferno, the only one of his drawings for the Divine Comedy which is in color. There is a Crucifixion by Pinturicchio which is the principal ornament of a Barberini Missal. Of the same period is another illumination of the Ottobonian Pontificate by Giovanni Vitez, concerning the Consecration of a Bishop. From the second half of the sixteenth century there is a first page of Dante's Paradise from an Urbino manuscript; another manuscript from Urbino shows a view of St. Mark's Square in Venice, etc. Among the drawings we may note a sketch by Raphael, and among the many autographs, of St. Thomas Aquinas, Petrarch, Henry VIII of England, Luther, T. Tasso, etc., we find a fragment of Michelangelo's Canzoniere. These names and examples are enough to give an idea of the incomparable treasures the Vatican Library has accumulated through the centuries for the scientific an artistic nourishment of mankind.

Miniature from the Joshua Roll - Miniatura del Rótulo de Josué
Miniature du rouleau de Josué - Miniatura del rotulo di Giosuè

La Biblioteca Vaticana es la colección bibliográfica más importante del mundo, no por el número, sino por el valor de sus códigos, que abrazan a todas las fases y a todos los aspectos de la civilización. A la importancia del contenido añádese el esplendor del ambiente, cuya hermosura puede compararse con la de la Galería de los Mapas, descrita arriba.

Un ejemplo típico del genéro es el Salón Sixtino (cerca de $70 \times 15$ metros) que, dividido en dos naves por dos hileras de pilares, ocupa el piso superior del palacio encargado por Sixto V, a través del patio de Belvedere. El salón está completamente cubierto de frescos, que desarrollan al asunto de la glorificación del libro y de las empresas edilicias y urbanisticas que imortalizaron el nombre de aquel Pontífice.

Sobre los grandes pilares están las figuras míticas de los inventores del alfabeto; sobre las paredes laterales, de un lado, están representadas las Bibliotecas más afamadas de la historia, y, del otro lado, los Concilios de la Iglesia que guardan a las verdades custodiadas en los libros. Más arriba, en los lunetos debajo de la bóveda, están representadas las obras monumentales cumplidas por Sixto V dentro del breve período de cinco años que transformaron el aspecto de Roma y marcaron a los rasgos de su arreglo moderno. Sobre unas mesas colocadas entre los pilares, preciosas por sus mármoles y bronces, están expuestos presentes principescos y autógrafos de importancia especial. Pero la riqueza mayor está en los escaparates alineados en la nave de tra-

Miniature from the Vatican Virgil - Miniatura del Virgilio Vaticano
Miniature du Virgile du Vatican - Miniatura del Virgilio Vaticano

montana, donde pueden admirarse los códigos más preciosos y raros, desde el manuscripto más antiguo de la Biblia en la traducción griega de los Setenta, hasta la carta que el príncipe japonés Mutsu envió a Pablo V en 1613.

Aquí como muestras están reproducidas unas miniaturas del código del Virgilio Vaticano y del Rótulo de Josué, que representan las últimas pruebas del arte clásica del IV y V siglo d. de C. y el pasaje al arte bizantina del VII y VIII siglo. De valor extraordinario es la miniatura del Canto XIV del Infierno de Dante, por Botticelli, el único en colores de los dibujos ejecutados por él para la Divina Comedia. Hay una Crucifixión de Pinturicchio, que es el adorno sobresaliente de un Misal Barberini. Contemporánea a esta hay otra miniatura del Pontifical Ottoboniano por Giovanni Vitez, que ilustra a la consagración de un Obispo. A la segunda mitad de 1500 deben atribuirse la primera página del Paraíso de Dante de un código urbinate de la Divina Comedia, así como una página de otro código urbinate con una vista de la Plaza San Marco de Venecia, etc.

Entre los dibujos obsérvase un esbozo de Rafael y, entre los numerosos autógrafos, los de San Tomás de Aquino, de Petrarca, de Enrique VIII de Inglaterra, de Lutero, de Torquato Tasso, etc., además de un trozo del cancionero de Miguel Ángel. Llegan estes nombres y estas citaciones para dar una idea de los tesoros inestimables que la Biblioteca Vaticana vino acumulando en los siglos para el nutrimiento científico y artístico de la humanidad.

Miniature from the Codex of Frederick II - Miniatura del Código de Federico II
Miniature du code de Frédéric II - Miniatura del Codice di Federico II

La Bibliothèque Vaticane est la collection bibliographique la plus importante du monde entier, sinon pour le nombre du moins pour la valeur de ses codes qui embrassent toutes les phases et tous les aspects de la civilisation. A l'importance du contenu se joint la magnificence du décor, les salles d'exposition qui le disputent pour la beauté des ornements et pour les sujets traités dans les peintures à la Galerie des Cartes Géographiques. Un exemple typique du genre est la grande Salle Sixtine (env. 70 m. × 15) qui, divisée en deux nefs par des piliers, occupe l'étage supérieur du palais ordonné par Sixte-Quint à travers la cour du Beldévère. Elle est d'un bout à l'autre couverte de fresques qui développent les sujets de la glorification du livre et des entreprises publiques (urbanisme et voirie) qui ont immortalisé le nom de ce hardi pontife.

Sur de grands piliers se dressent les figures mythiques des inventeurs de l'alphabet; sur les murs latéraux, d'un côté sont représentées les plus célèbres bibliothèques de l'histoire, et de l'autre les Conciles de l'Eglise qui ont défendu la vérité gardée dans les livres; plus haut, dans les lunettes placées sous la voûte, sont représentées les oeuvres monumentales accomplies par ce même Pape dans le bref laps de cinq années, qui ont transformé le visage de Rome et tracé les grandes lignes de sa configuration moderne. Sur les tables disposées entre les piliers, précieuses par leurs bronzes et leurs marbres, sont exposés les dons princiers et les autographes d'une importance particulière. Mais ce qu'il y a de plus riche est dans les vitrines alignées le long de la nef nord, où l'on peut admirer les codes les plus précieux et les plus rares, depuis le plus

217

Fresco of the Cavalcade of Sixtus V - Fresco de la cabalgada de Sixto V
Fresque de la chevauchée de Sixte-Quint - Affresco della cavalcata di Sisto V

ancien manuscrit de la Bible dans la version grecque des Septante, jusqu'à la lettre du prince japonais Mutsu à Paul V (1613).

A titre d'échantillon une reproduction est offerte ici de quelques miniatures du code du Virgile Vatican et du Rouleau de Giosué, qui permettent de voir les derniers essais de l'art classique du IV^e et du V^e siècle aprés J. C., et la transition à l'art byzantin du VII-VIII^e siècle. Une miniature du XIV^e chant de l'Enfer de Dante par Botticelli revêt une extrême importance, car c'est la seule en couleurs qu'il ait laissée d'après ses dessins de la Divine Comédie. Une Crucifixion de Pinturicchio constitue le principal ornement du Missel Barberini. Une autre miniature, qui se rapporte à la consécration d'un évêque, celle du *Pontificalis Ottobonianus* de Jean Vitez, est contemporaine de la précédente. Et c'est à la seconde moitié du XVI^e siècle que remontent la première page du Paradis de Dante d'un code urbinate de la Divine Comédie, et une autre page d'un code urbinate avec vue de la Place Saint-Marc à Venise.

Parmi les dessins on peut signaler une esquisse de Raphaël et parmi les nombreux autographes de saint Thomas d'Aquin, de Pétrarque, de Henri VIII d'Angleterre, du Tasse, de Luther, etc., un passage du manuscrit poétique de Michel-Ange. Il suffit de ces noms et citations pour donner une idée des trésors incomparables que la Bibliothèque Vaticane a accumulés au cours des siècles pour la nourriture scientifique et artistique de l'humanité.

Fresco of the Library at Jerusalem - Fresco de la Biblioteca de Jerusalén
Fresque de la Bibliothèque de Jérusalem - Affresco della Biblioteca di Gerusalemme

La Biblioteca Vaticana è la raccolta bibliografica più importante di tutto il mondo, se non per il numero, per la preziosità dei suoi codici che abbracciano tutte le fasi e tutti gli aspetti della civiltà. All'importanza del contenuto si accompagna lo splendore dell'ambiente, le sale d'esposizione che possono competere, per bellezza degli ornati e per i temi trattati nelle pitture, con la già descritta galleria delle Carte Geografiche. Esempio tipico del genere è il Salone Sistino (circa m. 70×15) che, diviso da pilastri in due navate, occupa il piano superiore del palazzo ordinato da Sisto V attraverso il cortile di Belvedere. Esso è da capo a fondo ricoperto di affreschi, i quali svolgono i temi della glorificazione del libro e delle imprese edilizie ed urbanistiche che hanno immortalato il nome dell'animoso pontefice.

Sui grandi pilastri sono le figure mitiche degli inventori dell'alfabeto; sulle pareti laterali da una parte sono rappresentate le più celebri Biblioteche della storia, e dall'altra i Concili della Chiesa che hanno la verità custodita nei libri; più in alto, nelle lunette sottostanti alla volta, sono rappresentate le opere monumentali compiute dal Pontefice medesimo nel breve giro di cinque anni, le quali hanno trasformato il volto di Roma e segnate le vie fondamentali della sua moderna configurazione. Sulle tavole frapposte ai pilastri, preziose di marmi e di bronzi, sono esposti doni principeschi ed autografi di speciale importanza. Ma la ricchezza maggiore sta nelle vetrine allineate nella navata di tramontana, dove si possono ammirare i codici più preziosi e rari, dal più antico mano-

Miniature from the Codex Ottobonianus - Miniatura del Código Ottoboniano
Miniature du Code Ottobonien - Miniatura del Codice Ottoboniano

scritto della Bibbia nella versione greca dei Settanta, fino alla lettera del principe giappo-
nese Mutsu a Paolo V del 1613.

Qui come saggio sono riprodotte alcune miniature del codice del Virgilio Vaticano e
del Rotulo di Giosuè, con le quali si vedono le ultime prove dell'arte classica
del IV e del V secolo dopo C. e il passaggio all'arte bizantina del VII-VIII sec.
Di straordinaria importanza è la miniatura del XIV canto dell'Inferno di Dante, di
Botticelli, l'unica a colori dei disegni della Divina Commedia che egli ha lasciato.
Vi è una Crocefissione del Pinturicchio, che è il principale ornamento di un messale
Barberini. Contemporanea a questa vi è un'altra miniatura del Pontificale Ottoboniano
di Giovanni Vitez, che si riferisce alla consacrazione di un Vescovo. Alla seconda metà
del '500 vanno riferite la prima pagina del Paradiso di Dante, di un codice urbinate
della Divina Commedia, ed una pagina di altro codice urbinate con una veduta della
Piazza San Marco a Venezia, ecc.

Tra i disegni si può notare uno schizzo di Raffaello, e tra i molti autografi, di S. Tommaso d'Aquino, del Petrarca, di Enrico VIII d'Inghilterra, di Lutero, di T. Tasso,
ecc., un brano del canzoniere di Michelangelo. Bastano questi nomi e queste citazioni
a dare un'idea dei tesori incomparabili che la Biblioteca Vaticana ha accumulato nei
secoli per il nutrimento scientifico ed artistico dell'umanità.

Pinturicchio: Miniature representing the Crucifixion - Pinturicchio: Miniatura con la Crucifixión
Pinturicchio: Miniature représentant la Crucifixion - Pinturicchio: Miniatura con la Crocefissione

221

Miniature from the Gospel Book of Lorsch - Miniatura del Evangeliario de Lorsch
Miniature de l'Evangéliaire de Lorsch - Miniatura dell'Evangeliario di Lorsch

Miniature for a Divine Comedy - Miniatura para una Divina Comedia
Miniature pour une Divine Comédie - Miniatura per una Divina Commedia

Miniature representing a Procession of a Doge in Venice - Miniatura con Procesión Dogal a Venecia
Miniature représentant la procession du Doge à Venise - Miniatura con processione dogale a Venezia

THE MUSEO SACRO AND THE MUSEO PROFANO

LOS MUSÉOS SACRO Y PROFANO

MUSÉE RELIGIEUX ET MUSÉE PROFANE

I MUSEI SACRO E PROFANO

The Aldobrandini Wedding (detail) - Las Nupcias Aldobrandini (detalle)
Les noces Aldobrandini (détail) - Le nozze Aldobrandini (particolare)

With the names Sacro and Profano we distinguish two collections annexed to the Library which, though small, are of inestimable value for the treasures they contain and because they were the first of all the Vatican Museums. Actually, the Vatican Library set the example; and here, as in many great Abbeys and Monasteries, the love of books brought the veneration of the arts and sciences, especially of history, which left its trace in inscriptions, coins and medals, and in all those little objects that accompany the lives of men from the cradle to the grave, in the intimacy of family life as well as in the pomp of civic and religious rites. In the process of time the small collections grew, making other similar and more imposing foundations necessary; but the first collections always remained in the same place, increased in authority and renown, and carefully kept in the peaceful and quiet atmosphere preferred by scholars. The Museo Sacro came into being in 1756 on the southern side of the wing of the Library, facing the Gardens; and eleven years later the Museo Profano was inaugurated on the northern side.

Goldsmith's works, coins, glasses, objects of domestic use and religious objects form the nucleus of these collections. In the last century the Museo Profano became even more important with the acquisition of ancient mural paintings of the Augustan era discovered among the ruins of Rome and Ostia, among which the most noteworthy are the so-called Aldobrandini Wedding, a series of episodes from the Odyssey and two graceful scenes of children in a procession. Among the treasures kept in the Museo Sacro are a priceless ivory diptych of the eighth century from the monastery of Rambona, and the enameled cross of the Sancta Sanctorum, whose patterned silver casket is here reproduced.

Procession of Children from Ostia - Procesión de niños de Ostia
Procession d'enfants d'Ostie - Processione di fanciulli da Ostia

Con los nombres de Muséos Sacro y Profano indícanse dos colecciones anexadas a la Biblioteca, de tamaño reducido pero de valor inestimable debido a los monumentos que incluyen, monumentos que abrieron el camino a todos los demás Muséos Vaticanos. Con efecto, el primer ejemplo fué dado por la Biblioteca Vaticana. Aquí como en otros lugares, en las grandes abadías como en las catedrales, el culto de los libros engendraba la pasión para las artes y la sabeduría, y especialmente de la historia, que tenía sus manifestaciones directas en las inscripciones, en las monedas y en las medallas, así como en todos aquellos objetos menudos que acompañan al hombre desde el nacimiento hasta la tumba, en la intimidad de su familia así como en la pompa de las solemnidades públicas, civiles o religiosas. En proceso de tiempo las pequeñas colecciones aumentaron, determinando más fundaciones semejantes y más grandiosas; pero no dejaron de existir las primeras, mejoradas y de mayor autoridad y fama, pero siempre custodiadas cuidadosamente en el recogimiento y en la paz, condiciones, estas, esenciales y preferidas por los hombres de estudio.

Fué así constituido en 1756 el Museo Sacro en la extremidad meridional del ala de la Biblioteca que mira hacia los Jardines, y, once años más tarde, el Museo Profano, en el ala septentrional. El núcleo principal de los dos Muséos está representado por joyerías, monedas, vidrios, y objetos de empleo casero y de culto. En el siglo pasado el Muséo Profano tuvo un fomento extraordinario debido a la colección de las pinturas murales antiguas de la Edad augustal, descubiertas entre las ruinas de Roma y de Ostia, entre las cuales destácanse las así llamadas « Nupcias Aldobrandini », una serie de episodios de la Odisea y dos hermosas escenas de niños en procesión y en acto de rezar. Entre los tresoros custodiados en el Muséo Sacro hay un precioso díptico de marfil del siglo VIII proveniente del monasterio de Rambona, y la Cuz esmaltada del « Sancta Sanctorum », del cual reproducimos aquí la teca de custodia en plata repujada.

228

Procession of Children from Ostia - Procesión de niños de Ostia
Procession d'enfants d'Ostie - Processione di fanciulli da Ostia

Par ces mots de religieux et profane on désigne deux collections annexées à la Bibliothèque, petites d'extension, mais d'une valeur inestimable quant aux monuments qui en font partie et qui ont frayé la voie à tous les autres Musées du Vatican. C'est la Bibliothèque Vaticane qui a donné en effet le premier exemple. Ici, comme ailleurs, dans les grandes abbayes et auprès des cathédrales, le culte du livre engendrait celui des arts et du savoir, avant tout de l'histoire, qui avait ses manifestations directes dans les inscriptions, dans les monnaies et médailles et dans tous les menus objets qui accompagnent la vie de l'homme du berceau à la tombe, aussi bien dans l'intimité de sa vie de famille que dans la pompe des solennités publiques, civiles et religieuses. Au cours des âges, les petites collections augmentèrent, déterminèrent d'autres fondations analogues et plus grandioses, mais les premières restèrent en place, améliorées et accrues en fait d'autorité et de renommée, gardées avec un soin jaloux dans leur recueillement et leur paix, conditions requises par les hommes d'études.
C'est ainsi qu'en 1756 le Musée religieux fut ouvert à l'extrémité méridionale de l'aile de la Bibliothèque donnant sur les Jardins, et onze ans plus tard le Musée profane du côté septentrional. Orfèvreries, monnaies, vitraux, objets d'usage domestique et du culte en forment le noyau principal. Au siècle passé le Musée profane eut un extraordinaire développement grâce aux peintures murales antiques de l'époque d'Auguste retrouvées dans les ruines de Rome et d'Ostie, parmi lesquelles il convient de signaler celles qui sont connues sous le nom de Noces Aldobrandini, une série d'épisodes de l'Odyssée et deux gracieuses scènes d'enfants en procession et priant. Au nombre des trésors gardés dans le Musée religieux se trouve un précieux diptyque en ivoire du VIIIe siècle provenant du Monastère de Rambona, et la Croix émaillée du Sancta Sanctorum dont le reliquaire de garde en argent repoussé a été reproduit dans ce volume.

Ulysses among the Laestrygonians - Ulises entre los Lestrígones
Ulysse chez les Lestrygons - Ullisse fra i Lestrigoni

Coi nomi di Sacro e Profano si distinguono due collezioni annesse alla Biblioteca, piccole di estensione, ma di valore inestimabile per i monumenti che ne fanno parte e che hanno preparato la strada a tutti gli altri Musei Vaticani. La Biblioteca Vaticana ha dato infatti il primo esempio. Qui, come altrove, nelle grandi abbazie e presso le cattedrali, il culto del libro generava quello delle arti e del sapere, anzitutto della storia, che aveva le sue manifestazioni dirette nelle iscrizioni, nelle monete e medaglie ed in tutti quegli oggetti minuti che accompagnano la vita dell'uomo dalla nascita alla tomba, così nell'intimità della famiglia come nella pompa delle solennità pubbliche, civili e religiose. In processo di tempo le piccole raccolte aumentarono, determinando altre fondazioni analoghe e più grandiose; ma rimasero al loro posto le prime, migliorate e cresciute di autorità e di fama, custodite scrupolosamente nel raccoglimento e nella pace, condizioni preferite dagli uomini di studio.

Così sorse nel 1756 il Museo Sacro nell'estremità meridionale dell'ala della Biblioteca prospiciente i Giardini, ed undici anni dopo il Museo Profano nel lato settentrionale. Oreficerie, monete, vetri, oggetti di uso domestico e di culto ne formano il nucleo principale. Nel secolo scorso il Museo Profano ebbe uno straordinario incremento con la raccolta di pitture murali antiche d'età augustea, rinvenute nelle rovine di Roma e di Ostia, fra cui vanno segnalate le così dette *Nozze Adobrandine*, una serie di episodi dell'Odissea e due graziose scene di fanciulli in processione ed oranti. Fra i tesori custoditi nel Museo Sacro trovasi un pregevole dittico di avorio del sec. VIII proveniente dal monastero di Rambona, e la Croce smaltata del *Sancta Santorum*, della quale qui si riproduce la teca di custodia in argento sbalzato.

230

Ivory  Diptych  of  Rambona - Díptico  de  marfil  de  Rambona
Diptyque  en  ivoire  de  Rambona - Dittico  eburneo  di  Rambona

Casket of the Enameled Cross of the Sancta Sanctorum - Teca de la Cruz esmaltada del Sancta Sanctorum
Etui reliquaire émaillé du Sancta Sanctorum - Teca della Croce smaltata del Sancta Sanctorum

232

THE RECEPTION HALLS

LAS SALAS DE RECEPCIÓN

LES SALLES DE RÉCEPTION

LE SALE DI RICEVIMENTO

The Royal Hall - Sala Regia - Salle Royale - Sala Regia

In the apartments of the Popes there was always a large hall for the reception of groups of cardinals or important delegations. In the Borgia Apartment the Hall of the Popes was used for this purpose; in the apartment of Julius II it was the Hall of Constantine. Later on, with the enlarging of the palace and the increase in the number of visitors seeking an audience, the need was felt for halls with a larger capacity and with decorations which would be more in accord with the dignity of the Pope. The oldest of these halls are the Royal Hall, where Emperors, Kings and their ambassadors were received, and the Ducal Hall, where the dukes and their representatives were admitted. The Royal Hall, constructed by the younger Giuliano da Sangallo under Paul III, has a vault decorated with moldings by Perin del Vaga, Daniele da Volterra and Sansovino. The side walls, under Pius V and Gregory XIII, were covered with fourteen frescoes by the greatest masters of the time, known as the *manieristi*: Giorgio Vasari, Taddeo Zuccari, Giuseppe Salviati, etc., who painted the temporal achievements of the Roman Papacy, from the first struggles with the Germanic invaders to the battle of Lepanto. From the Royal Hall we pass — in front of the Sistine Chapel — to the Ducal Hall which results from two separate halls: the dividing wall was substituted by Bernini

235

The Ducal Hall - Sala Ducal - Salle Ducale - Sala Ducale

with an arch covered with moldings. The lunettes and the vaults of this hall were decorated under Popes Pius IV, Pius V and Gregory XIII by the Bolognese Lorenzo Sabbatini and other artists of the time, among them the two Flemish painters, Paul and Matthew Brill.

Other receptions halls, in the Papal apartment proper, are the Clementine and the Consistorial Halls.

The Clementine Hall, the first on entering the apartment and protected by the Swiss Guard, owes its name to Clement VIII who had it adorned with marble and decorated with frescoes in 1595 by Giovanni Alberti, assisted by his brother Cherubino and by Paul Brill. These frescoes represent the life and martyrdom of St. Clement the Pope. Built near the Clementine not much later, the Consistorial Hall has a remarkably rich ceiling. All around, on the upper part of the walls, Paul Brill painted the most famous Italian hermitages of the time, and Alberti depicted the Saints who had dwelt there. Last of the reception halls, because it is outside the Papal apartment, is the Hall of the third Loggia of Gregory XIII, who dedicated it to Bologna; of this hall we have already spoken in the chapter on the Palace.

236

The Clementine Hall - Sala Clementina - Salle Clémentine - Sala Clementina

En los aposentos de los Pontífices hubo siempre alguna sala más amplia para recibir a los Cardenales, a las deputaciones y a las embajadas más numerosas. En el aposento Borja había una Sala, llamada «de los Pontífices», para este uso; en el aposento de Julio II era la sala de Constantino. Más tarde, al ensancharse el Palacio y al aumentar el número de los visitantes que pedían audiencia, se reparó la necesidad de salas de mayor capacidad, cuyas decoraciones se armonizasen mejor con la dignidad del Pontífice. Las más antiguas de estas salas son la Sala Regia y la Sala Ducal. En la primera recibíanse a los Emperadores, a los Reyes y a sus embajadores, siendo la Sala Ducal para los Ducas de mayor potencia y para sus apoderados. La primera fué encargada por Pablo III a Giuliano de Sangallo el jóven, y fué adornada de estucos por Perin del Vaga, por Daniele de Volterra y por el Sansovino. Las paredes laterales, bajo Pio V y Gregorio XIII, fueron pintadas a fresco con 14 cuadros en que rivalizaron los mejores maestros de aquella epoca, conocidos bajo el nombre genérico de «manieristas»: Giorgio Vasari, Taddeo Zuccari, Giuseppe Salviati, etc., que representaron los faustos temporales del Pontificado romano, desde las primeras luchas con los Longobardos hasta la batalla de Lépanto.

Desde la Sala Regia pásase, enfrente de la Capilla Sixtina, a la Sala Ducal, que resultó

The Consistorial Hall - Sala del Consistorio
Salle du Concistoire - Sala del Concistoro

de dos cámaras separadas por una pared cuando esta fué derribada por Bernini y re-
emplazada por un gran arco disfrazado con un apanamiento de estuco. Los lunetos
y las bóvedas de estas salas fueron adornadas bajo los Papas Pio IV, Pio V y Gregorio XIII por el boloñes Lorenzo Sabbatini y por otros artistas de la época, entre
quienes dos flamencos, Pablo y Mateo Brill. Otras salas de recepción, en el aposento
pontificio mismo, son la Sala Clementina y la Sala del Consistorio.
La Sala Clementina, que es la primera después del ingreso del aposento, y está custo-
diada por Guardas Suizos, tomó su nombre de Clemente VIII encargó su revestimiento
con mármoles y su decoración con frescos a Giovanni Alberti (1595) con la ayuda de su
hermano Cherubino y de Pablo Brill, que representó el martirio de San Clemente Papa.
Próxima a la Sala Clementina, y posterior a esta de uños años (fué completada en 1603)
hay la Sala del Consistorio, con un techo riquísimo. Alrededor de la sala, en la parte
superior de las paredes, Pablo Brill pintó a las romerías italianas más afamadas de aquel
tiempo, y Alberti a las figuras de los Santos que allí habian vivido.
Ultima de las salas de recepción, por estar fuera del aposento pontificio, es la Sala
de la tercera Logia de Gregorio XIII, que quizo dedicarla a Boloña, y de que ya hemos
hablado en el párrafo relativo al Palacio.

The Bologna Hall (back wall) - Sala de Boloña (pared de fondo)
Salle de Bologne (paroi de fond) - Sala di Bologna (parete di fondo)

Dans les appartements des Pontifes il y a toujours eu quelque salle plus vaste, dans laquelle étaient reçus les cardinaux en corps ou les députations et les ambassades plus nombreuses. Dans l'appartement des Borgia cette salle était appelée Salle des Pontifes, dans celui de Jules II, Salle de Constantin. Plus tard, à mesure que le palais s'étendit, et avec l'augmentation des visiteurs qui demandaient audience, le besoin se fit sentir de salles plus vastes et dont les décorations fussent davantage en harmonie avec la dignité du Souverain Pontife. Les plus anciennes de ces salles sont la Royale et la Ducale. Dans la Salle Royale on recevait les empereurs, les rois et leurs ambassadeurs, tandis que dans la Salle Ducale étaient reçus les ducs « di maggior potenza » et leurs invités. La Salle Royale, construite sur ordre de Paul III par Giuliano da San Gallo le jeune, eut sa voûte décorée de stucs de Perin del Vaga, Daniel de Volterra et Sansovino. Les murs latéraux furent peints de fresques par un groupe de peintres de manière, comme Giorgio Vasari, Taddeo Zuccari, Giuseppe Salviati, etc., représentant les grandeurs temporelles du Pontificat romain, depuis les premières luttes avec les Lombards j'usqu'à la bataille de Lépante.

De la Chapelle Royale on passe — en face de la Chapelle Sixtine — à la Salle Ducale

The Bologna Hall (ceiling) - Sala de Boloña (techo) - Salle de Bologne (plafond) - Sala di Bologna (soffitto)

qui est la résultante de deux salles séparées par une cloison que Bernini remplaça par un grand arceau masqué d'une draperie en stuc.

Les lunettes et les voûtes de cette salle furent décorées sous les papes Pie IV, Pie V et Grégoire XIII par le Bolonais Lorenzo Sabbatini et par d'autres artistes du temps, parmi lesquels les deux Flamands Paul et Mathieu Brill.

Il y a comme autres salles de réception, dans l'appartement pontifical proprement dit, la Salle Clémentine et celle du Concistoire.

La Salle Clémentine, la première à l'entrée de l'appartement et gardée par la Garde Suisse, reçoit son nom de Clément VIII qui la fit revêtir de marbres et décorer de fresques en 1595 par Giovanni Alberti, assisté de son frère Cherubino et de Paul Brill, qui y représenta la vie et le martyre du pape saint Clément. Non loin de la Clémentine et de quelques années postérieure (achevée en 1603) est la Salle du Concistoire au très riche plafond. Tout autour, dans la zone supérieure des murs, Paul Brill a peint les ermitages italiens les plus célèbres de l'époque, et l'Alberti les figures des saints qui y avaient séjourné. La dernière des salles de réception, car elle est en dehors de l'appartement pontifical, est la salle de la troisième loge de Grégoire XIII, qui la voulut dédiée à Bologne, et dont il a déjà été question dans le chapitre des Palais.

The Hall of the Paraments - Sala de los Paramentos - Salle des Parements - Sala dei Paramenti

Negli appartamenti dei Pontefici vi fu sempre qualche sala più vasta, nella quale erano ricevuti i Cardinali in corpo, o le deputazioni e le ambascerie più numerose. Nell'Appartamento Borgia era questa la sala detta dei Pontefici; nell'appartamento di Giulio II era la sala di Costantino. Più tardi, con l'estendersi del palazzo e con l'aumento dei visitatori che domandavano udienza, si sentì il bisogno di sale di maggior capacità e che con le loro decorazioni si accordassero meglio con la dignità del Pontefice. Le più antiche di queste sale sono la Regia e la Ducale. Nella sala Regia si ricevevano gli imperatori, i re e i loro ambasciatori; laddove nella sala Ducale i duchi « di maggior potenza » e i loro inviati. La sala Regia costruita per ordine di Paolo III da Giuliano da Sangallo il giovane, fu decorata nella volta di stucchi di Perin del Vaga, Daniele da Volterra e dal Sansovino. Le pareti laterali, sotto Pio V e Gregorio XIII, furono affrescate con quattordici quadri, in cui gareggiarono i migliori maestri del tempo, noti col nome generico di manieristi: Giorgio Vasari, Taddeo Zuccari, Giuseppe Salviati, ecc., che vi hanno rappresentate le grandezze temporali del Pontificato romano, dalle prime lotte coi Longobardi alla battaglia di Lepanto.
Dalla sala Regia si passa — di fronte alla Cappella Sistina — alla sala Ducale, che è la risultante di due sale separate da una parete sostituita dal Bernini con un grande

The Hall of the Secret Consistory - Sala del Consistorio secreto
Salle du Concistoire secret - Sala del Concistoro segreto

arco mascherato da un drappeggio di stucco. Le lunette e le volte di questa sala furono decorate sotto i Papi Pio IV, Pio V e Gregorio XIII dal bolognese Lorenzo Sabbatini e da altri artisti del tempo, tra i quali i due fiamminghi, Paolo e Matteo Brill. Altre sale di ricevimento, nell'appartamento pontificio vero e proprio, sono la Clementina e quella del Concistoro.

La sala Clementina, la prima all'ingresso dell'appartamento e custodita dalla Guardia Svizzera, prende il nome da Clemente VIII che la fece rivestire di marmi e decorare di affreschi nel 1595 da Giovanni Alberti, assistito dal fratello Cherubino e da Paolo Brill, che vi rappresentò la vita e il martirio di S. Clemente papa. Vicino alla Clementina e di pochi anni posteriore (ultimata nel 1603) è la sala del Concistoro, dal ricchissimo soffitto. Tutto in giro, nella zona superiore delle pareti, Paolo Brill dipinse i romitaggi italiani più celebri in quel tempo, e l'Alberti le figure dei Santi che vi avevano fatto dimora.

Ultima delle sale di ricevimento, perchè fuori dell'appartamento pontificio, è la sala della terza loggia di Gregorio XIII, che la volle dedicata a Bologna, e della quale si è già parlato nel capitolo sul Palazzo.

242

THE PINACOTECA

LA PINACOTECA

LA PINACOTHÈQUE

LA PINACOTECA

The Pinacoteca is of fairly recent origin, as it was inaugurated only after 1815, when the works of art which had been carried off from Rome and the Papal State during the French invasion of 1797 were finally returned from Paris. It changed its location many times, until Pius XI settled it definitely in the palace built, under the direction of the architect Luca Beltrami, near the new entrance to the Museums (1932). The Vatican collection complements the works which the great masters of the Renaissance left in the Chapels, Halls, Stanze and Galleries, and reveals new aspects of their activity. It would not be possible, for example, to have an exact idea of Raphael's genius if, besides his frescoes, we could not see the Madonna di Foligno, the Transfiguration, and the Tapestries woven from his cartoons. In the same way, our knowledge of primitive art is greatly increased by the works of the Florentine, Sienese and Umbrian masters, and by the Stefaneschi Altar of Giotto, which we find in the first halls of the Pinatocea, and above all, by that unique eleventh century painting of the Last Judgment. And what good fortune for the lover of beauty to have here, reunited in one room, the greater part of the frescoes by Melozzo da Forlì which were saved when the Apsis of the Blessed Apostles was demolished, and the fresco of the Founding of the Vatican Library, left for so many years on the ground floor of Nicholas V's palace! Add to these Leonardo's St. Jerome, Titian's Madonna dei Frari, Domenichino's Communion of St. Jerome, Caravaggio's Deposition, Murillo's Marriage of St. Catherine, etc., and we realize that the Vatican Pinacoteca is much more than an appendix: judged essentially for the value of its works, it may be considered as an independent organism which is a perennial source of study and artistic enjoyment for everyone.

It is true that the Pinacoteca has a special character, in that its pictures are almost all by Italian artists and on religious subjects. But we may point out that Italian art has always had a predominant place; and as regards the religious contents of the paintings, the history of religion, from the Biblical tales to the legends with which popular fantasy has embellished the lives of the Saints, is such a rich source of happy and sad themes, that it has always inspired a great variety of works of art, highly appreciated by sensitive and cultivated people.

La Pinacoteca tiene orígenes bastante recientes, pues fué inaugurada tán solo despues de 1815, cuando volvieron de Paris obras hurtadas de Roma y del Estado Pontificio durante la invasión francesa de 1797; la Pinacoteca cambió su sede varias veces, hasta que Pio XI la alojó definitivamente en el palacio edificado en el jardín, cerca del nuevo ingreso de los Museos (1932), bajo la dirección del arquitecto Luca Beltrami. La colección Vaticana debe considerarse como el complemento natural de las Galerías de Pintura. Los grandes Maestros del Renacimiento que se admiran en la Capilla del Angélico, en la Sixtina, en las Salas Borja, en las Cámaras y en las demás Galerías, hallan aqui un precioso aditamento en los cuadros que repiten a sus nombres o revelan a un nuevo aspecto de su actividad. Sería posible tener una idea exacta del genio de Rafael si, además de sus frescos, no pudiéramos ver aquí su Madona de Foligno, la Transfiguración y los Tapices tejidos bajo sus cartones? Y que contribución ofrecen a nuestro conocimento del arte primitiva los maestros florentinos, seneses, umbro-marquesanos y el altar Stefaneschi de Giotto que podemos ver en las primeras salas de la Pinacoteca y, primera entre todos, y única en su género, la gran tabla de Juicio Universal del siglo XI. Y que dicha para los estudiosos hallar aquí, aunados en una sala, la mayoría de los frescos de Melozzo de Forlí salvados de la demolición de la ábsida de la Iglesia de los Apóstoles, y el fresco de la fundación de la Biblioteca Vaticana, guardada por tantos siglos en los cuartos del piso bajo del Palacio de Nicolas V. Añádanse el San Jerónimo de Leonardo, la Madona de San Nicolò dei Frari de Ticiano, la Ultima Comunión de San Jerónimo de Domenichino, le Deposición de la Cruz de Caravaggio, las Nupcias de Santa Catalina de Murillo, etc., se y comprenderá fácilmente que la Pinacoteca Vaticana, aún, bajo ciertos aspectos, pueda parecer más bien un apéndice, juzgandola essencialmente por el valor de sus obras, puede verdaderamente ser considerada una entidad independiente y una fuente perennal de estudio y de deleite artístico para todos.

No escapará a nadie su carácter especial por ser casi todos sus cuadros hechos por artístas italianos y de asunto religioso; pero ni la italianidad ni la religiosidad pueden considerarse una verdadera imperfección, pues el arte italiana gozó siempre la primacía sobre la de las demás naciones de Europa, y la religiosidad no puede significar pobreza de inspiración o de forma, pués la historia religiosa, desde las simples narraciones bíblicas hasta las leyendas con que la fantasía del pueblo quizo embellecer a la vida de los Santos, presenta una variedad tal de escenas tristes y alegres, que el artísta puede hallar en ella, como siempre halló, una mina riquísima de asuntos para su paleta y para el gusto de los visitadores imparciales y de gran cultura.

La Pinacothèque a des origines assez récentes, car elle fut inaugurée seulement après 1815 quand les œuvres soustraites à Rome et à l'Etat pontifical par l'invasion des armées napoléoniennes en 1797 revinrent de Paris, et elle changea de local plusieurs fois jusqu'à ce que Pie XI la fit aménager d'une façon définitive dans le palais érigé dans le jardin, près de la nouvelle entrée des Musées (1932), sous la direction de l'architecte Luca Beltrami. La collection vaticane doit être considérée comme le complément naturel des Galeries de Peinture. Les grands maîtres de la Renaissance que l'on admire dans la chapelle de Fra Angelico, dans la Sixtine, dans les salles Borgia, dans les « Stanze » et les autres Galeries, trouvent ici un complément précieux avec les tableaux qui répètent leur nom ou révèlent un nouvel aspect de leur activité. Serait-il possible d'avoir une idée exacte du génie de Raphaël, si à côté de ses fresques nous ne pouvions voir ici la Madone de Foligno, la Transfiguration et les tapisseries tissues d'après ses cartons? Et quelle contribution n'apportent pas à notre connaissance de l'art primitif les maîtres florentins, siennois, ceux de l'Ombrie et des Marches et l'autel Stefaneschi de Giotto, qui nous sourient dès les premières salles de la Pinacothèque et, avant tous, unique en son genre, le grand tableau sur bois du Jugement Dernier remontant au XI$^e$ siècle ! Et quelle chance pour les amants du beau que d'avoir ici réunies dans une salle la plupart des fresques de Melozzo da Forlì sauvées de la démolition de l'abside des Saints-Apôtres, et celle de la fondation de la Bibliothèque Vaticane, restée durant des siècles au palais de Nicolas V dans les salles du rez-de-chaussée! Ajoutons encore le Saint Jérôme de Léonard, la Madone de S. Nicolò de' Frari du Titien, la dernière communion de saint Jérôme du Dominiquin, le Christ déposé de la Croix du Caravage, le Mariage de sainte Catherine de Murillo, et l'on comprendra aisément que si la Pinacothèque Vaticane semble à la réflexion une sorte d'appendice, jugée essentiellement d'après la valeur des œuvres qu'elle renferme, elle peut être considérée comme un organisme indépendant, source intarissable d'études et de jouissances artistiques pour la communauté.

Il n'échappera à personne qu'elle est d'un caractère particulier du fait que ses tableaux sont presque tous d'artistes italiens et de sujet religieux. Mais ni l'italianité ni la religiosité ne peuvent sérieusement être jugés un défaut, l'art italien ayant toujours bénéficié d'une primauté sur celui des autres nations d'Europe; et sa religiosité ne peut signifier pauvreté d'inspiration ou de forme, puisque l'histoire religieuse, des simples récits bibliques aux légendes dont l'imagination populaire a embelli la vie des saints, offre une telle variété de scènes tristes et gaies, que l'artiste y peut trouver, comme d'ailleurs il l'a toujours fait, une mine extrêmement riche de sujets pour sa palette et pour les délices des visiteurs impartiaux et de large culture.

La Pinacoteca ha origini abbastanza recenti, perchè fu inaugurata soltanto dopo il 1815, quando ritornarono da Parigi le opere trafugate da Roma e dallo Stato Pontificio per l'invasione francese del 1797, e mutò sede più volte, fino a che Pio XI le diede una sistemazione definitiva nel palazzo eretto nel Giardino, presso il nuovo ingresso dei Musei (1932), sotto la direzione dell'architetto Luca Beltrami. La collezione Vaticana deve considerarsi come il naturale complemento delle Gallerie di Pittura. I grandi maestri del Rinascimento che si ammirano nella Cappella dell'Angelico, nella Sistina, nelle sale Borgia, nelle Stanze e nelle altre Gallerie, trovano qui un prezioso complemento nei quadri, che ripetono il loro nome o rivelano un nuovo aspetto delle loro attività. Sarebbe possibile avere idea esatta del genio di Raffaello, se accanto ai suoi affreschi non potessimo veder qui la Madonna di Foligno, la Trasfigurazione e gli Arazzi tessuti sulla base dei suoi cartoni? E quale contributo apportano alla nostra conoscenza dell'arte primitiva i maestri fiorentini, senesi, umbro-marchigiani e l'altare Stefaneschi di Giotto che ci sorridono nelle prime sale della Pinacoteca, e, avanti a tutti, unica nel suo genere, la grande tavola del Giudizio Universale dell'XI secolo! E quale fortuna per l'amante del bello aver qui riuniti in una sala la maggior parte degli affreschi di Melozzo da Forlì salvati dalla demolizione dell'abside dei SS. Apostoli, e quello della fondazione della Biblioteca Vaticana, rimasto per tanti secoli nei locali a pianterreno del palazzo di Nicolò V! Si aggiungono il S. Girolamo di Leonardo, la Madonna di S. Nicolò de' Frari del Tiziano, l'ultima Comunione di S. Girolamo del Domenichino, il Cristo deposto dalla croce del Caravaggio, lo Sposalizio di S. Caterina del Murillo, ecc., e si comprenderà facilmente che la Pinacoteca Vaticana, se per qualche riflesso appare come un'appendice, giudicata essenzialmente nel valore delle sue opere, può veramente considerarsi come un organismo indipendente, fonte perenne di studio e di godimento artistico per tutti.

Non sfuggirà ad alcuno che essa ha un carattere speciale nel fatto che i suoi quadri sono quasi tutti di artisti italiani e di argomento religioso. Ma nè l'italianità, nè la religiosità possono seriamente giudicarsi un difetto, perchè l'arte italiana ha goduto sempre di un primato sulle altre nazioni d'Europa, e la sua religiosità non può significare povertà d'ispirazione o di forma, perchè la storia religiosa dalle semplici narrazioni bibliche alle leggende di cui la fantasia popolare ha abbellito la vita dei Santi, presenta tale una varietà di scene tristi e liete, che l'artista vi può trovare, come vi ha trovato sempre, una miniera ricchissima di temi per la sua tavolozza e per la delizia dei visitatori imparziali e di larga cultura.

The Last Judgment (XI century) - Juicio Universal del siglo XI
Jugement Dernier du XIe siècle - Giudizio Universale dell'XI secolo

Giotto: *The Stefaneschi Triptych* (front) - Giotto: *Tríptico Stefaneschi* (recto)
Giotto: *Triptyque Stefaneschi* (recto) - Giotto: *Trittico Stefaneschi* (recto)

Giotto: *The Stefaneschi Triptych* (back) - Giotto: *Tríptico Stefaneschi* (verso)
Giotto: *Triptyque Stefaneschi* (verso) - Giotto: *Trittico Stefaneschi* (verso)

250

Giotto: *The Stefaneschi Triptych* (detail of the Redeemer) - Giotto: *Tríptico Stefaneschi* (detalle del Redentor)
Giotto: *Triptyque Stefaneschi* (détail du Rédempteur) - Giotto: *Trittico Stefaneschi* (particolare del Redentore)

251

Giotto: *The Stefaneschi Triptych* (detail of St. Peter) - Giotto: *Tríptico Stefaneschi* (detalle de San Pedro)
Giotto: *Triptyque Stefaneschi* (détail de saint Pierre) - Giotto: *Trittico Stefaneschi* (particolare di S. Pietro)

Beato Angelico: *Madonna with Child and Saints* - Beato Angélico: *Madona con Niño y Santos*
Fra Angelico: *Vierge avec l'Enfant Jésus et saints* - Beato Angelico: *Madonna col Bambino e Santi*

Beato Angelico: *St. Nicholas Saves a Boat from Shipwreck* - Beato Angélico: *San Nicolas salva una nave del naufragio*
Fra Angelico: *Saint Nicolas sauvant un bateau du naufrage* - Beato Angelico: *S. Nicolò salva una nave dal naufragio*

Masolino da Panicale: *The Crucifixion* - Masolino de Panicale: *Crucifixión*
Masolino da Panicale: *Crucifixion* - Masolino da Panicale: *Crocefissione*

Benozzo Gozzoli: *Madonna della Cintura* - Benozzo Gózzoli: *Madona del Cinturón*
Benozzo Gozzoli: *Vierge à la Ceinture* - Benozzo Gozzoli: *Madonna della Cintura*

Melozzo da Forlì: *The Founding of the Library* - Melozzo de Forlí: *Fundación de la Biblioteca*
Melozzo da Forlì: *Fondation de la Bibliothèque* - Melozzo da Forlì: *Fondazione della Biblioteca*

257

Melozzo da Forlì: *The Founding of the Library* (detail with the Portrait of Platina)
Melozzo de Forlí: *Fundación de la Biblioteca* (detalle con el retrato de Platina)
Melozzo da Forlì: *Fondation de la Bibliothèque* (détail avec le portrait du Platina)
Melozzo da Forlì: *Fondazione della Biblioteca* (particolare con il ritratto del Platina)

Melozzo da Forlì: *Angel* - Melozzo de Forlí: *Ángel músico*
Melozzo da Forlì: *Ange musicien* - Melozzo da Forlì: *Angelo musicante*

Melozzo da Forlì: *Angel* - Melozzo de Forlí: *Ángel músico*
Melozzo da Forlì: *Ange musicien* - Melozzo da Forlì: *Angelo musicante*

260

Melozzo da Forlì: *Angel* - Melozzo de Forlí: *Ángel músico*
Melozzo da Forlì: *Ange musicien* - Melozzo da Forlì: *Angelo musicante*

Giovanni Bellini: *Pietà* - Giovanni Bellini: *Piedad*
Jean Bellin: *Pietà* - Giovanni Bellini: *Pietà*

Leonardo da Vinci: *St. Jerome* - Leonardo da Vinci: *San Jerónimo*
Leonard de Vinci: *Saint Jérôme* - Leonardo da Vinci: *S. Gerolamo*

Perugino: *Madonna and Saints* - Perugino: *Madona y Santos*
Perugin: *Vierge et Saints* - Perugino: *Madonna e Santi*

Raphael: *The Annunciation* - Rafael: *Anunciación*
Raphaël: *Annonciation* - Raffaello: *Annunciazione*

Raphael: *The Circumcision* - Rafael: *Circuncisión*
Raphaël: *Circoncision* - Raffaello: *Circoncisione*

Raphael: *The Adoration of the Magi* (detail) - Rafael: *Adoración de los Reyes Magos* (detalle)
Raphaël: *Adoration des Mages* (détail) - Raffaello: *Adorazione dei Magi* (particolare)

Raphael: *Madonna di Foligno* - Rafael: *La Madona de Foligno*
Raphaël: *La Madone de Foligno* - Raffaello: *La Madonna di Foligno*

Raphael: *Madonna di Foligno* (detail) - Rafael: *La Madona de Foligno* (detalle)
Raphaël: *La Madone de Foligno* (détail) - Raffaello: *La Madonna di Foligno* (particolare)

Raphael: *The Transfiguration* - Rafael: *La Transfiguración*
Raphaël: *La Transfiguration* - Raffaello: *La Trasfigurazione*

Raphael: *The Transfiguration* (detail) - Rafael: *La Transfiguración* (detalle)
Raphaël: *La Transfiguration* (détail) - Raffaello: *La Trasfigurazione* (particolare)

Raphael: *The Transfiguration* (detail) - Rafael: *La Transfiguración* (detalle)
Raphaël: *La Transfiguration* (détail) - Raffaello: *La Trasfigurazione* (particolare)

Titian: *Madonna dei Frari* - Ticiano: *Madona dei Frari*
Titien: *Madone des Frari* - Tiziano: *Madonna dei Frari*

Barocci: *The Rest on the Flight into Egypt* - Barocci: *Descanso durante la fuga en Egypto*
Barocci: *Repos pendant la fuite en Egypte* - Barocci: *Riposo durante la fuga in Egitto*

273

Domenichino: *The Communion of St. Jerome* (detail) - Domenichino: *Comunión de San Jerónimo* (detalle)
Le Dominiquin: *Communion de Saint Jérôme* (détail) - Domenichino: *Comunione di S. Gerolamo* (particolare)

Caravaggio: *The Deposition* - Caravaggio: *Deposición*
Caravage: *La Déposition* - Caravaggio: *Deposizione*

Murillo: *The Marriage of St. Catherine* - Murillo: *Nupcias de Santa Catalina*
Murillo: *Mariage de sainte Cathérine* - Murillo: *Sposalizio di S. Caterina*

THE MUSEUMS

LOS MUSÉOS

LES MUSÉES

I MUSEI

The Museums are a most eloquent index of the high consideration that the Roman Papacy has always had for the monuments of classic antiquity in which it recognized a ray of the eternal light of truth and beauty. Statues, terra-cottas, bronzes and inscriptions were collected in the Vatican from the dawn of the Renaissance, and the Museo Sacro and the Museo Profano of the Library were established. But, as separate institutions and in their own appropriate premises, the Museums had their origin and development under Popes Clement XIV (1769-1774) and Pius VI (1775-1799).

Giovanni Battista and Ennio Quirino Visconti were charged with the task of selecting and arranging the art works, and the architects Simonetti and Camporesi were commissioned to adapt several halls in the old palaces for this use and to plan new buildings where necessary. In this way a splendid group of buildings was organized which, joining the northern wing of the Library with the Little Palace of Innocent VIII, gave life to the Museo Pio-Clementino. This museum, already in 1792, had more than 1440 art objects and was open to the public of scholars and art lovers.

In 1796 the Napoleonic invasion brought to a halt this fine undertaking, and with the treaty of Tolentino (1798), imposed by force of arms on Pius VI, an incalculable number of pictures, statues, ancient coins and medals, manuscripts and documents, took the road to France and went to enrich the Museums, Galleries and Libraries in Paris. Pius VII (1800-1823) sought to remedy these very grave losses, and as new treasures were brought to light by the excavations, he arranged at once the Museum called by his name Chiaramonti, which came to occupy the northern part of the Bramante Corridor. Interrupted by his deportation to France, the work was swiftly taken up again on his return and was completed with the erection of the Braccio Nuovo, on which Canova and the architect Raffaele Stern collaborated. In this way a new gallery arose, where, from the floor decorated with precious marbles and mosaics to the vaults, everything is attuned to a sense of peace and harmony that prepares the spirit for the enjoyment of art.

Gregory XVI (1831-1846) completed the work of his predecessors with the founding of the Etruscan Museum and the Egyptian Museum. Thus, thanks to the wise understanding and interest of these Popes, the Vatican Palace was able to offer to scholars of ancient civilization a group of galleries and halls which are in no way inferior to the most celebrated museums in Europe and America and where we find treasures, not only of Rome and Italy, but also of Greece and Egypt, the cardinal points, we may say, of archeology and art. Whoever needs proof has only to go through the illustrations of this volume, in which some of the most significant and most celebrated examples are reproduced.

Los Muséos son un índice muy elocuente de la elevada consideración con que el Pontificado Romano cuido siempre a los monumentos de la antiguedad clásica, por reconocer en ellos un rayo de la eterna luz de verdad y de belleza, siendo pues ellos dignos de consideración y respeto. Estátuas, terracotas, bronces e inscripciones comenzaron a ser recogidas en el Vaticano desde los primeros años del Renacimiento, y los Muséos Sacro y Profano son el reflejo natural de esta actividad; pero, como instituciones distinguidas de las demás y con sedes especiales y adecuadas, los Muséos, en el sentido más amplio de la palabra, tuvieron su orígen y desarrollo bajo los Pontificados de Clemente XIV (1769-1774) y de Pio VI (1775-1799).

Giovanni Battista y Ennio Quirino Visconti fueron encargados con escojer y colocar a los monumentos, mientras que los Arquitectos Simonetti y Camporesi tuvieron la tarea de adaptar para ellos unas salas en los viejos palacios y de proyectar, donde fuera menester, edificios nuevos. Erigióse así un magnífico cuerpo de edificios que, conectando el ala septentrional de la Biblioteca con el Palacete de Inocencio VIII, constituyó al Muséo Pio-Clementino; desde hace 1792 este muséo comprendia más que 1440 monumentos, tenía una guía imprimida y estaba abierto al público de los estudiosos de arte. La invasión napoleónica de 1796 paró al movimiento tán felizmente empezado; más bién, con el Convenio de Tolentino (1798) impuesto a Pio VI con la fuerza de las armas, un número inmenso de cuadros, estátuas, monedas antiguas y medallas, códigos y papeles de archivo tomaron el camino hacia Francia, y fueron enriquecer a los Muséos, a las Galerías y a las Bibliotecas de París. Pio VII (1800-1823) trató de remediar a pérdidas tán graves y, aprovechando de los monumentos llevados a la luz por las escavaciones, mandó luego edificar al Muséo que de su nombre fué llamado Muséo Chiaramonti, y que vino ocupar a la parte septentrional del Corredor de Bramante. La obra, interrumpida por su deportación a Francia, fué resumida activamente con su vuelta, y fué completada por la erección del Brazo Nuevo, donde colaboraron Canova y el arquitecto Rafael Stern. Edificóse así una nueva Galería donde, desde el suelo, decorado con mármoles preciosos, hasta los mosaicos de las bóvedas, todo esta armonizado con un sentido de paz y de proporción que prepara el espíritu a los verdaderos goces del arte.

Gregorio XVI (1831-1846) completó a la obra de sus antecesores edificando a más dos Muséos, dedicados a las antiguedades de Etruria y de Egypto. Así, debido al conocimiento y a la ayuda de estes Pontífices, el Palacio Vaticano pudo ofrecer a los estudiosos de las civilizaciones antiguas un conjunto de Galerías y de Salas que puede favorablemente sostener a la comparación con los más afamados muséos de Europa y de America, y donde se hallan custodiados monumentos no tán solo de Roma o de Italia, sino también de Grecia y de Egypto, que podemos llamar los punto cardinales de la Arqueología y del Arte. Y quien deseara la prueba de esto tiene tán solo que examinar a las láminas de este volúmen, donde están reproducidos unos de los ejemplares más significativos y afamados.

Les Musées sont un indice on ne peut plus éloquent de la haute estime dont le Pontificat Romain a toujours entouré les monuments de l'antiquité classique, dans lesquels on a reconnu un rayon de l'éternelle lumière de vérité et de beauté, dignes par conséquent de considération et de respect. Statues, terres cuites, bronzes et inscriptions commencèrent à être collectionnés au Vatican dès l'aube de la Renaissance et les Musées Religieux et Profane de la Bibliothèque en sont le reflet naturel; toutefois en tant qu'institutions distinctes des autres et ayant leurs sièges spéciaux et appropriés, les Musées, au sens le plus large du mot, naquirent et se développèrent sous le Pontificat de Clément XIV (1769-1774) et de Pie VI (1775-1779).

Giovanni Battista et Ennio Quirino Visconti furent chargés de choisir et de classer les monuments, et les architectes Simonetti et Camporesi d'adapter pour ceux-ci quelques salles des anciens palais, et de dresser les plans de nouveaux édifices en cas de besoin. C'est ainsi que fut organisé un corps magnifique de bâtiments qui reliant l'aile septentrionale de la Bibliothèque au Petit Palais d'Innocent VIII, donna lieu au Musée Pio Clementino, qui dès 1792 comptait plus de 1440 monuments, possédait un guide imprimé et était ouvert au public des hommes d'études et des amateurs d'art.

L'invasion napoléonienne de 1796 arrêta cet essor si bien heureux, et bien plus, avec le traité de Tolentino (1798) imposé par la force des armes à Pie VI, un nombre incalculable de tableaux, statues, monnaies antiques et médailles, de codes et de papiers d'archives prirent le chemin de la France et allèrent enrichir les Musées, les Galeries et les Bibliothèques de Paris.

Pie VII (1800-1823) chercha à remédier à des pertes aussi graves, et profitant des monuments mis à jour par les fouilles, organisa aussitôt le Musée qui prit son nom de Chiaramonti et vint occuper la partie nord du « corridor » de Bramante. L'œuvre, interrompue par la déportation du Pape en France, fut reprise activement à son retour et complétée par l'érection de la nouvelle aile (Braccio Nuovo) à laquelle collaborèrent Canova et l'architecte Raphaël Stern. Une autre galerie surgit de la sorte où, depuis le pavement décoré de marbres précieux et de mosaïques jusqu'aux voûtes, une impression de calme et d'harmonie est partout répandue et prépare l'esprit aux pures délectations de l'art.

Grégoire XVI (1831-1846) compléta l'œuvre de ses prédécesseurs avec la fondation de deux Musées nouveaux destinés aux antiquités de l'Etrurie et de l'Egypte. Grâce à la sage compréhension et à la faveur de ces pontifes, le Palais du Vatican peut offrir à ceux qui étudient les civilisations antiques un ensemble de galeries et de salles qui ne le cède en rien aux Musées les plus célèbres d'Europe et d'Amérique, et où sont gardés avec soin les monuments non seulement de Rome et de l'Italie, mais aussi de la Grèce et de l'Egypte, que l'on peut appeler les points cardinaux de l'Archéologie et de l'Art. Quiconque en désiderait les preuves n'a qu'à parcourir les planches de ce volume où sont reproduits quelques-uns des exemplaires les plus significatifs et les plus en renom.

I Musei sono un indice eloquentissimo dell'alta considerazione in cui il Pontificato Romano ha tenuto sempre i monumenti dell'antichità classica, nei quali si riconobbe un raggio dell'eterna luce di verità e di bellezza, meritevoli perciò di considerazione e di rispetto. Statue, terrecotte, bronzi ed iscrizioni cominciarono a raccogliersi in Vaticano fino dagli albori del Rinascimento ed i Musei Sacro e Profano della Biblioteca ne sono il naturale riflesso; ma, come istituti distinti dagli altri e con sedi speciali loro appropriate, i Musei, nel senso più ampio della parola, ebbero origine e sviluppo sotto il Pontificato di Clemente XIV (1769-1774) e di Pio VI (1775-1799).

Giovanni Battista ed Ennio Quirino Visconti ebbero l'incarico della scelta e dell'ordinamento dei monumenti, e gli architetti Simonetti e Camporesi quello di adattare per essi alcune sale dei vecchi palazzi, e di progettare, dov'era necessario, nuovi edifici. Così fu organizzato uno splendido corpo di fabbricati, che, congiungendo l'ala settentrionale della Biblioteca col Palazzetto d'Innocenzo VIII, diede vita al Museo Pio Clementino, il quale fino dal 1792 contava più di 1440 monumenti, possedeva una guida a stampa ed era aperto al pubblico degli studiosi e degli amatori d'arte.

L'invasione napoleonica nel 1796 arrestò il movimento così felicemente iniziato, chè anzi col trattato di Tolentino (1798) imposto con la forza delle armi a Pio VI, un numero incalcolabile di quadri, statue, monete antiche e medaglie, di codici e di carte d'archivio presero la via della Francia e andarono ad arricchire i Musei, le Gallerie e le Biblioteche di Parigi. Pio VII (1800-1823) cercò di rimediare a perdite così gravi, ed approfittando dei monumenti messi in luce dagli scavi, ordinò subito il Museo detto dal suo nome Chiaramonti, che venne ad occupare la parte settentrionale del « corridore » di Bramante. L'opera, interrotta dalla sua deportazione in Francia, fu ripresa alacremente al suo ritorno, ed ebbe compimento coll'erezione del Braccio Nuovo, a cui collaborarono il Canova e l'architetto Raffaele Stern. Sorse in tal modo una nuova galleria, dove, dal pavimento decorato di marmi preziosi e di mosaici alle volte, tutto è intonato ad un senso di calma e di armonia che prepara lo spirito ai veri godimenti dell'arte.

Gregorio XVI (1831-1846) completò l'opera dei suoi predecessori con la fondazione di due nuovi Musei, destinati alle antichità dell'Etruria e dell'Egitto. Così grazie al saggio intendimento e al favore di questi pontefici, il Palazzo Vaticano potè offrire agli studiosi delle civiltà antiche un complesso di gallerie e di sale che non cede al confronto coi più celebrati Musei dell'Europa e dell'America, e dove sono custoditi monumenti non solo di Roma e dell'Italia, ma anche della Grecia e dell'Egitto, che si possono chiamare i punti cardinali dell'Archeologia e dell'Arte. Chi ne desiderasse le prove non ha che percorrere le tavole di questo volume, in cui sono riprodotti alcuni degli esemplari più significativi e più celebrati.

The Round Hall - La Sala Redonda - Salle Ronde - La Sala Rotonda

The Gallery of the Candelabra - La Galería de los Candelabros
Galerie des Candélabres - La Galleria dei Candelabri

The Braccio Nuovo - El Brazo Nuevo
Le Braccio Nuovo (Nouvelle aile) - Il Braccio Nuovo

Queen Tewe - La Reina Tewe - La Reine Tewe - La Regina Tewe

The Naophorus - El Naóforo - Le Naophore - Il Naoforo

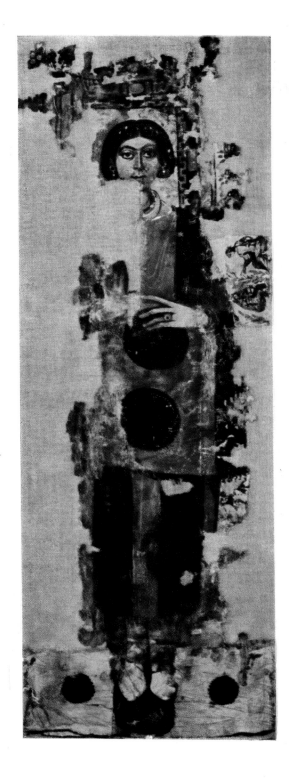

Mummy's cover - Cubierta de momia - Couverture de momie - Copertura di mummia

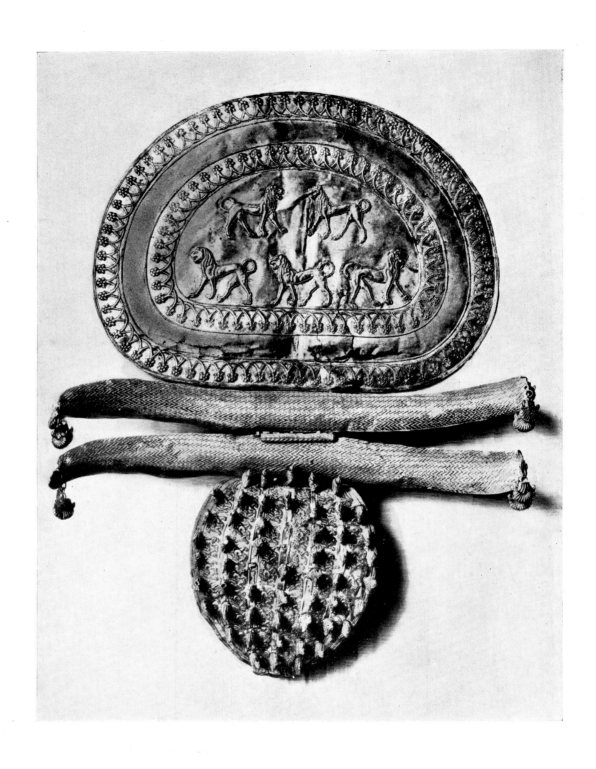

Gold Fibula from the Regolini-Galassi Tomb - Fíbula de oro de la tumba Regolini-Galassi
Fibule d'or du tombeau Regolini-Galassi - Fibula d'oro della tomba Regolini-Galassi

Amphora of Exechias (front) - Anfora de Exechias (recto)
Amphore d'Exechias (recto) - Anfora di Exechias (recto)

Amphora of Exechias (back) - Anfora de Exechias (verso)
Amphore d'Exechias (verso) - Anfora di Exechias (verso)

White-Ground Crater with Polychrome Figures - Cratera de fondo blanco con figuras polícromas
Cratère, fond blanc avec figures polychromes - Cratere a fondo bianco con figure policrome

291

Dying  Hunter  (terra-cotta)  -  Cazador  muribundo  (terracota)
Chasseur mourant (terre-cuite) - Cacciatore morente (terracotta)

292

The Mars of Todi (bronze) - El Marte de Todi (bronce)
Le Mars de Todi (bronze) - Il Marte di Todi (bronzo)

The Mars of Todi (detail) - El Marte de Todi (detalle)
Le Mars de Todi (détail) - Il Marte di Todi (particolare)

The Jove of Otricoli - El Jupiter de Otricoli
Le Jupiter d'Otricoli - Il Giove di Otricoli

The Nile - El Nilo - Le Nil - Il Nilo

The Sleeping Ariadne - Ariana adormecida
Ariane endormie - Arianna addormentata

Bust of Pericles - Busto de Péricles
Buste de Périclès - Busto di Pericle

297

Girl Running - Niña que sale corriendo
Jeune fille prenant son élan pour la course - Fanciulla che si slancia alla corsa

298

Apollo Belvedere - Apolo de Belvedere
Apollon du Belvédère - Apollo di Belvedere

Torso of Belvedere - Tronco del Apolo de Belvedere
Torse du Belvédère - Torso del Belvedere

300

Satyr with Infant Bacchus - Sátiro con Dióniso niño
Satyre avec Dionysos enfant - Satiro con Dioniso bambino

Demosthenes - Demóstenes - Demosthènes - Demostene

Laocoön - Laocoonte - Laocoon - Laocoonte

Head of Laocoön - Cabeza del Laocoonte - Tête du Laocoon - Testa del Laocoonte

The Augustus of Prima Porta - Augusto de Primera Puerta
Auguste de Prima Porta - Augusto di Prima Porta

305

The Flavian Reliefs - Relieves Flavios - Reliefs des Flaviens - Rilievi Flavii

The Vibian Family - La Familia Vibio - La Famille Vibio - La famiglia Vibio

The procession of the «Dii Compitales» - Procesión de los «Dii Compitales»
Procession des «Dii Compitales» - Processione dei «Dii Compitales»

Giotto: *The Angel of the Navicella* (mosaic) - Giotto: *Ángel de la Navecilla* (mosaico)
Giotto: *Ange de la Navicella* (mosaïque) - Giotto: *Angelo della Navicella* (mosaico)

# INDEX OF THE ILLUSTRATIONS

# ÍNDICE DE LAS ILUSTRACIONES

# TABLE DES ILLUSTRATIONS

# INDICE DELLE ILLUSTRAZIONI

# INDEX OF THE PHOTOGRAPHS
## ÍNDICE DE LAS FOTOGRAFÍAS
## INDEX DES PHOTOS
## REFERENZE FOTOGRAFICHE

Alinari - Firenze: 56 a - 59 - 81 - 122 a - 156 - 182 - 230 - 231 - 262 - 292 - 307 a - 308

Anderson - Roma: 25 - 34 - 37 - 38 - 39 - 40 - 41 - 42 - 43 - 47 - 48 - 49 - 50 - 51 - 55 - 57 - 58 - 60 - 85 - 86 - 87 - 88 - 89 - 90 - 91 - 92 - 96 - 99 - 100 - 102 - 103 - 104 - 105 - 106 - 108 - 110 - 112 - 113 - 114 - 116 - 118 - 120 - 122 b - 124 - 126 - 128 - 133 - 134 - 136 - 138 - 144 - 145 - 146 - 147 - 148 - 149 - 150 - 154 - 162 - 163 - 164 - 166 - 167 - 168 - 170 - 172 b - 173 b - 174 - 180 - 186 - 187 - 188 - 189 - 190 - 194 - 195 - 196 - 199 - 228 - 254 - 258 - 260 - 264 - 266 - 268 - 270 - 271 - 272 - 274 - 276 - 285 - 293 - 294 - 295 - 296 a - 297 - 298 - 299 - 300 - 303 - 304 - 305.

Archivio Fotografico Musei Vaticani: 82 - 157 - 185 - 215 - 219 - 222 - 240 - 249 - 250 - 256 - 263 - 286 - 288 - 301 - 306 - 307 b.

Bruni - Roma: 21.

Brunner & C. - Como: 13.

Heilbronner - Berlino: 56 b.

Fotocelere - Torino: 296 b.

Istituto Enciclopedia Italiana - Roma: 14.

Istituto Italiano d'Arti Grafiche - Bergamo: 5 - 17 - 93 - 94 - 95 - 101 - 107 - 109 - 111 - 115 - 117 - 119 - 121 - 123 - 125 - 127 - 135 - 137 - 139 - 140 - 143 - 151 - 153 - 155 - 158 - 161 - 165 - 169 - 171 - 172 a - 173 a - 175 - 176 - 177 - 178 - 179 - 181 - 193 - 200 - 201 - 202 - 203 - 204 - 205 - 206 - 207 - 208 - 209 - 210 - 211 - 221 - 223 - 227 - 229 - 251 - 253 - 255 - 257 - 259 - 261 - 265 - 267 - 269 - 273 - 275 - 287 - 289 - 291.

Rotalfoto - Milano: 33.

Sansaini - Roma: 29 - 35 - 36 - 44 - 45 - 46 - 52 - 53 - 54 - 63 - 67 - 71 - 75 - 79 - 80 - 152 - 214 - 216 - 217 - 218 - 220 - 224 - 232 - 235 - 236 - 237 - 238 - 239 - 241 - 242 - 252 - 283 - 284 - 290 - 302.

FINITO DI STAMPARE
NELLE OFFICINE DELL'ISTITUTO ITALIANO D'ARTI GRAFICHE
DI BERGAMO
IL 30 LUGLIO 1950